Contents

Section I   Introduction

Section II   Overview of the Treaty of Amsterdam

Section III   Detailed Account of the Treaty of Amsterdam

Section I

Introduction

CHAPTER ONE

The purpose of the White Paper

1.1   The aim of this White Paper is to explain as clearly as possible the changes which will be made in the European Union and in the European Communities by the Treaty of Amsterdam, 1997.

1.2   The European Union of today has been created and shaped by a series of treaties negotiated between the Member States over a period of nearly fifty years. Since Ireland, along with the UK and Denmark, joined the European Communities in 1973, further Accession Treaties admitted Greece, Spain, Portugal, Sweden, Austria and Finland to membership; the Single European Act of 1986 established the Single Market; and the Maastricht Treaty of 1992 established the European Union (of which the European Communities form part) and set the framework for Economic and Monetary Union.

1.3   The latest step in this process is the negotiation and signature of the new Treaty of Amsterdam. Like its predecessors, the Single European Act and the Maastricht Treaty, the new Treaty is the outcome of an intensive negotiation between the Member States of the Union at an Intergovernmental Conference (IGC).

How the Treaty was negotiated

1.4   The task of negotiating the Treaty at this Conference of Member States was entrusted by the Heads of State or Government to their Foreign Ministers. The detailed preparatory work was carried out under their direction by a negotiating group consisting of a representative of each of the fifteen Foreign Ministers and a representative of the President of the Commission. The Heads of State or Government and the President of the Commission reviewed progress at successive meetings of the European Council (including two held in Dublin in the second half of 1996).

Timetable of the Conference

1.5   The Conference opened at Foreign Minister level at Turin on 29 March 1996 under the chairmanship of Italy which held the Presidency of the European Union at that time. It continued under Irish chairmanship during the Irish Presidency in the second half of 1996; and Ireland had the task of producing the first draft for the new Treaty at the end of its Presidency in December 1996. The Heads of State or Government at the European Council meeting in Dublin on 13/14 December 1996 approved the Irish outline draft as a good basis for further work.

1.6   The work of the Conference continued under the Netherlands Presidency in the first half of 1997. It culminated in Amsterdam on 16/17 June 1997 when the Heads of State or Government approved a text for the new Treaty. After some further technical legal work to prepare the text in due form for signature, the new Treaty was signed by the Foreign Ministers in a ceremony at Amsterdam on 2 October 1997.

Ratification of the Treaty

1.7   The new Treaty of Amsterdam will come into effect only if it is ratified by all fifteen Member States of the Union. In most Member States, ratification will depend on Parliamentary approval. In some Member States the approval of the electorate will also be sought through a referendum.

Referendum in Ireland

1.8   At the European Council meeting in Amsterdam on 16/17 June, the then Taoiseach, Mr. John Bruton T.D., joined on behalf of Ireland in approving the outcome of the negotiations. The then Minister for Foreign Affairs, Mr. Ray Burke T.D., signed the new Treaty on behalf of Ireland in Amsterdam on 2 October 1997.

1.9   Subject to the passage of the necessary Bill by the Dáil and the Seanad, a referendum which will take the form of a proposal to amend the Constitution will be held in Ireland in Spring 1998. Referenda on similar lines were held in 1972 to ratify Ireland's entry to the European Communities; in 1987 to allow Ireland to ratify the Single European Act; and in 1992 to allow it to ratify the Treaty of Maastricht.

1.10   The exact wording of the Constitutional amendment which will be put to the people in Spring 1998 has not yet been decided. In effect, however, in the referendum, the Government will be seeking the approval of the people for the new Treaty.

The need to make the Treaty understood

1.11   When they embarked on the negotiation of the new Treaty the Governments of the Member States expressed their particular concern that the Union and its institutions should be brought closer to the citizens of the Member

States so that the peoples of the Union would have a sense of ownership and participation in the structures established in their name and for their benefit.

1.12   When it fell to Ireland to prepare and submit a first draft for the new Treaty in December 1996 towards the end of the Irish Presidency, every effort was made to ensure that the text would be readable and comprehensible. The Netherlands took over the Presidency in January 1997 and maintained this approach for the remainder of the negotiations.

1.13   Almost inevitably, however, a Treaty, especially one which amends a series of earlier Treaties as this new Treaty does, must be expressed in technical, legal language. This was necessary also in the present case. The text as agreed in June 1997 had to be put into correct legal format for signature as a Treaty on 2 October. In consequence, the Treaty text as signed, although it remains the only authentic legal text, is not at first sight easy to read: in addition to new material which is relatively accessible, it includes also a large number of additions, deletions and cross references which are difficult to follow without close study of previous Treaty texts.

1.14   This makes it all the more important that the content of the Treaty and the changes and amendments which it proposes to make in the existing Treaties, should be adequately explained. That is the purpose of the present White Paper. It is right and necessary that the changes be fully understood by the Irish people who are being asked to accept them and by all of the citizens of the Union, in whose name and on whose behalf they were negotiated.

CHAPTER TWO

The Structure of the Treaties

General

2.1 Treaties are organised in numbered **Articles.** Articles may be grouped together in **Chapters**. A **Title** is, in principle, a larger sub-division of a Treaty which may contain a number of articles or even chapters — though it may also be as short as a single article. A Treaty may also have various **Sections.**

The Structure of the European Union

2.2 The legal structure of the European Union is very complex and it may be helpful at the outset to explain the interlocking character of the Treaties which have shaped it.

2.3 The **European Union** is the over-arching structure which includes the **European Communities**. It came into being formally as a result of the **Treaty on European Union** signed at Maastricht in 1992.

2.4 The European Union as structured by the Maastricht Treaty can be said to rest on three "Pillars": the **European Communities; the Common Foreign and Security Policy** (CFSP); and **Justice and Home Affairs** (JHA). (The term "Pillar" does not appear in the Treaty but it has now become common usage). These are explained further in the following paragraphs.

2.5 The <u>**First Pillar**</u>, though normally spoken of in the singular, actually comprises three legally separate entities — the three **European Communities**. These are respectively the **European Community** (EC), the **European Coal and Steel Community** (ECSC), and the **European Atomic Energy Community** (Euratom). The EC (European Community) was formerly known as the EEC (European Economic Community).

2.6   Each of these three Communities is the subject of a separate founding Treaty and each has a distinct international legal personality. The European Union as such, however, does not itself have an international legal personality.

2.7   The three European Communities share common institutions (the European Parliament, the Council, the Commission, the Court of Justice etc.) since the Merger Treaty entered into force in 1967, but there are certain legal differences in the way the three Communities operate. The common institutions in their actions on any issue follow the rules set by the Treaty governing the particular Community for which they are acting on that issue.

2.8   Each of the three Communities, which collectively comprise the First Pillar, is supra-national in character. The Treaties under which they operate (which are described as "primary legislation"), together with the acts of the institutions adopted in accordance with their provisions, (usually described as "secondary legislation") and the case law of the European Court of Justice constitute binding Community law for the Institutions, the Member States and their citizens.

2.9   The **Second Pillar** set up by the Maastricht Treaty is the **Common Foreign and Security Policy** (CFSP). The **Third Pillar** is **Cooperation in the fields of Justice and Home Affairs** (JHA). These two "Pillars" are different in character from the First Pillar in that they are not supra-national but retain much of the character of intergovernmental cooperation. The obligations they impose do not constitute Community law but they bind the Member States as a matter of Treaty law.

The Treaty of Amsterdam 1997 — form and structure

What the new Treaty will do

2.10   The Treaty of Amsterdam, although legally a separate Treaty, is not, in the ordinary sense of the words, a "stand-alone" Treaty. It is entirely directed to changing and adapting the provisions of the existing Treaties (i.e. the Treaty on European Union and the three Treaties on which the European Communities are based) as well as certain related Acts.

2.11   Most of the changes made affect either the Treaty on European Union (signed at Maastricht in 1992) or the Treaty establishing the European Community (one of the constituent parts of the First Pillar). In this White Paper the former is referred to either as "the EU Treaty" or, more colloquially, as "the Maastricht Treaty"; the latter is referred to as "the EC Treaty". Some of the changes made to the EC Treaty, however, particularly those affecting the shared institutions, will apply also to the Treaties establishing the two other Communities (the European Coal and Steel Community and the European Atomic Energy Community). This will be indicated appropriately in this White Paper wherever it is the case.

2.12   The changes which the new Treaty make will affect all three "Pillars" of the Union: the "First Pillar" (Community); the "Second Pillar" (Common Foreign and Security Policy) and the "Third Pillar" (Cooperation in Justice and Home Affairs). The "Third Pillar" (i.e. Justice and Home Affairs) will also be re-named. It is described formally in the new Treaty as *"Provisions on Police and Judicial Cooperation in Criminal Matters"*.

The Treaty as published

2.13   The text of the new Treaty is available in a document published by the Office for the Official Publications of the European Communities in Luxembourg. This document also contains the Final Act of the Intergovernmental Conference at which the Treaty was negotiated.

Final Act of the Conference

2.14   "Final Act" is the term used for the concluding document which is agreed at the end of an Intergovernmental Conference of this kind. The Final Act in the present case contains all of the texts adopted at the Conference, including the new Treaty, the new Protocols which are to be annexed to the existing Treaties and the Declarations made by Member States in regard to it. It has been signed by the Foreign Ministers on behalf of their respective Heads of State (and in the case of Ireland on behalf of the Presidential Commission which exercised the powers of the President at the time).

Layout of the Treaty

2.15   The Treaty itself has 15 Articles, organised in three Parts as follows:

Part 1 (Articles 1-5) Substantive Amendments
This part of the Treaty sets out the amendments to be made to the four Treaties and to the 1976 Act on direct elections to the Parliament.

Article 1
Amendments to the Treaty on European Union

Article 2
Amendments to the EC Treaty

Article 3
Amendments to the European Coal and Steel Community Treaty

Article 4
Amendments to the Euratom Treaty

Article 5
Amendments to the 1976 Act on European Parliament elections

Part 2 (Articles 6-11) Simplification

This part of the Treaty sets out in six Articles the amendments to the various Treaties and Protocols annexed to them which are necessary in order to delete certain lapsed provisions of those instruments without changing their legal effects and to make the necessary consequential changes.

Part 3 (Articles 12-15) General and Final Provisions

This part of the Treaty provides for the re-numbering of articles, titles and sections in the Treaty on European Union and the Treaty establishing the European Community. It also provides that the new Treaty is concluded for an unlimited period; that it shall enter into force at the beginning of the second month after all Member States have ratified it; and that the texts as signed in twelve languages (which include Irish) will all be equally authentic.

"Table of equivalences"

2.16   Since Part 2 of the new Treaty provides for a simplification of the existing Treaties by deleting articles which are now obsolete and Part 3 provides for a re-numbering of the articles in two of the Treaties, it is necessary to be clear about how the new and the old numbering of articles correspond to each other. This is shown by means of a "Table of Equivalences" which is attached as an Annex to the Treaty and legally forms part of it. The "Table of Equivalences" is reproduced as Appendix A to this White Paper for ease of reference.

Protocols

2.17   In addition to its other provisions as set out above, the new Treaty includes thirteen new Protocols. These will be annexed to the various existing Treaties (one to the EU Treaty only; four to both the EU and EC Treaties; five to the EC Treaty only; and three to all three of the Community Treaties) A **Protocol** has exactly the same legal status as the Treaty to which it is attached. It can be thought of as analogous to a P.S. to a letter or, in legal terms, a codicil to a will. Once the new Treaty enters into force these Protocols are to be read for the future as legally part of the respective Treaties to which they are to be attached. (The Protocols to the new Treaty are listed in appendix D of the present White Paper).

Declarations

2.18   As well as the text of the new Treaty and the Protocols which it will annex to the existing Treaties, the Final Act also contains some fifty one Declarations adopted by the Conference and eight Declarations made by one or more Member States of which the Conference as a whole took note. (These are listed in Appendix E).

2.19   A **Declaration** is a statement of the political intentions of those who signed the Treaty in question. Unlike a Protocol, it does not have a legal status equivalent to the provisions of a Treaty. A Declaration adopted by the Conference as a whole, that is by all of the Member States jointly, obviously carries greater weight than one made to express their national positions by one or two or three Member States only.

Consolidated texts of the Treaties

2.20   As noted above, in addition to amending and adding to the existing Treaties in various ways, the new Treaty of Amsterdam will also delete obsolete articles and re-number in sequence all the remaining articles of the EU and the EC Treaties. Obsolete articles have been deleted from the Treaties establishing the other two Communities (Coal and Steel Community and Euratom) but these two Treaties have not been re-numbered.

2.21   These changes have been incorporated in new, consolidated versions of the Treaty on European Union (ie the Maastricht Treaty), and the EC Treaty respectively. These "consolidated" Treaty texts are useful for reference purposes but they do not have legal status. Only the new Treaty of Amsterdam as actually signed (in the format explained above), read together with the original Treaties and the other Treaties which have changed and amended them over the years, will carry authority as the authentic legal texts.

Section II

Overview of the Treaty

CHAPTER THREE

An outline of what the new Treaty will do

3.1   This section of the White Paper offers a summary of the salient points of the new Treaty of Amsterdam. It is not comprehensive. It is intended rather as an overview which will give a general sense of what the new Treaty is about. A more detailed account, which also covers other issues not touched on in this overview, will be found in the main part of the White Paper, that is in Section III.

Fundamental Rights

3.2   The new Treaty will add provisions to the EU (Maastricht) Treaty which will state explicitly for the first time that the Union is founded on certain principles: liberty, democracy, human rights and fundamental freedoms and the rule of law.

3.3   These are principles held in common by all the Member States and respect for them will now be required of applicants for membership as a condition for admission to the Union. As a corollary, the Treaties will now, for the first time also, contain sanctions provisions which could be invoked if any Member State, old or new, were to turn its back in a fundamental way on these principles.

3.4   The sanctions could involve suspension of voting rights. They would be invoked only in the extreme case of a *"serious and persistent breach"* of the principles. A determination to this effect would be made unanimously (except for the offending State) by the Council, meeting at the level of Heads of State or Government, with the assent of the European Parliament voting by a two thirds majority. The sanctions could then be imposed, or lifted, by qualified majority vote of the Council of Ministers .

Human Rights jurisdiction of the Court of Justice

3.5   The new Treaty will create an explicit Treaty basis for a principle which the Court of Justice has already applied in its jurisprudence. The Court has said that it regards compliance with human rights standards set by the European Convention on Human Rights (of the Council of Europe) and by the constitutional traditions common to the Member States as a necessary condition for the lawfulness of Community acts. The new Treaty will add a provision to the

EU Treaty which will explicitly require the Court, wherever it has jurisdiction, to apply these human rights standards in relation to acts of the institutions of the Union.

Non-discrimination

3.6 The new Treaty will clarify, develop and further extend the provisions of the EC Treaty on equality between men and women and on equal pay for equal work or work of equal value. Positive action to redress existing imbalances between the sexes will be permitted.

3.7 A new provision added to the EC Treaty will allow the Council, within the limits of the powers conferred on it by the Community, to take action against discrimination. The new Article provides that the Council, acting unanimously on a Commission proposal and after consulting the Parliament, may take appropriate action to combat discrimination based on sex, racial or ethnic origin, religion or belief, disability, age or sexual orientation.

Churches

3.8 In a Declaration the Member States commit the Union to respect the status of Churches and philosophical and non-confessional organisations under the national law of Member States.

Progressive establishment of an area of freedom, security and justice

3.9 This is one of the most substantial sections of the new Treaty. It sets the aim of freedom of movement throughout the Union, coupled with appropriate "flanking measures" dealing with external border controls, immigration, asylum as well as closer cooperation in fighting crime, especially international crime and organised crime.

3.10 A new Title (a major section of a Treaty) dealing with free movement of persons, and such related matters as immigration policy, visas, asylum policy and practice and judicial cooperation in civil matters will be added to the EC Treaty. It sets out a five year programme of action and details the measures to be adopted by the Council over that period.

3.11 The effect will be to transfer a large number of these issues from the largely intergovernmental framework of the Third Pillar (the Justice and Home Affairs provisions of the EU Treaty). They will now become a Community responsibility, dealt with supranationally under the EC Treaty (First Pillar). Many of the characteristics of the present intergovernmental cooperation will be retained initially but there will be a greater use of the Community methods and procedures (role of the Commission, voting procedures, role of the Court of Justice etc.) after the five year transition period.

3.12   The UK was unwilling to be bound by these provisions and obtained exemption. Ireland too has obtained special exemptions because of its concern to maintain the Common Travel Area with the UK. Two Protocols to be attached to the EC Treaty will accommodate the positions of both countries and their right to maintain the Common Travel Area between them will be formally recognised. Either country, on certain conditions, will be able to opt in to proposals when they are first brought forward, or to join later in measures which were adopted initially without its participation. A further Protocol will deal with the position of Denmark and grant it certain exemptions.

Schengen cooperation brought into the Treaty

3.13   A separate framework of intergovernmental cooperation known as the Schengen process after the town in Luxembourg where the agreement was signed, has developed outside the EU since 1985. It now involves thirteen Member States of the EU. It deals with border and immigration controls, policing and security issues, including narcotics, firearms and extradition matters. There is also a databank known as the Schengen Information System. The whole of these arrangements will now be brought within the framework of the Treaties. The provisions and decisions already agreed in Schengen cooperation will be allocated either to the EC (First Pillar) or the EU (Third Pillar) Treaties. A Protocol providing for these arrangements will be added to the EC and the EU Treaties.

3.14   For reasons related to UK positions on freedom of movement, and to the Common Travel Area between both countries, neither Ireland nor the UK participate in Schengen. Now that it is to be brought within the EU framework the two countries may, if they wish, continue not to take part. Either or both will, however, also be able to opt in to all or part of Schengen, subject to certain conditions.

3.15   These above-mentioned Protocols which will be added to the EC and EU Treaties and a declaration made by Ireland annexed to the Final Act, taken together, make it clear that Ireland's concern is to maintain the Common Travel Area between Ireland and the UK in order to maximise freedom of movement of persons into and out of Ireland; and that, subject to this, Ireland would wish to participate to the maximum extent possible.

3.16   New Member States joining the Union from now on, unlike Ireland and the UK, will not be allowed to opt out of the cumulative body of Schengen decisions as it will stand at the time they enter. During their negotiations for membership they will be obliged to commit themselves to accept these decisions in full.

Police and judicial cooperation in criminal matters

3.17   In response to widespread concern about terrorism, drugs and the activities of criminals across borders, the "Third Pillar" (Cooperation in Justice and Home Affairs) of the EU will be substantially re-structured so as to make cooperation between the police and the Courts of Member States in combating crime more effective. This area of cooperation will also be re-named — it is now to be described as "Police and Judicial cooperation in criminal matters".

3.18   A range of the issues previously dealt with in the Third Pillar will be transferred to the Community framework (see above). The list of crimes which are to be the subject of police and judicial cooperation under the re-structured Third Pillar will be clarified and expanded. It will now include, for example, trafficking in persons and offences against children as well as illicit arms trafficking.

3.19   There are extensive new provisions on police cooperation, both direct and through Europol. Europol itself is to be strengthened and developed so that it will be able to play a greater supportive role in the investigative process between Member States. There are new provisions also for judicial and customs cooperation in the fight against cross-border crime, organised or otherwise.

3.20   The decision-making procedures of the Third Pillar are also to be clarified and improved. The Court of Justice will have a more substantial role in this area and there will be a limited increase in the role of the European Parliament. There will also be a role for the Ombudsman. There are also new provisions which will give to the Union as such the capacity to conclude international agreements on matters dealt with under the Third Pillar. Operational expenditure incurred in implementing Third Pillar provisions will now be charged to the Community budget unless the Council, by unanimity, decides otherwise.

3.21   There will also be new Treaty provisions allowing "closer cooperation" ("flexibility"). This means that a number of Member States, provided they are at least a majority, may be authorised by a Council decision to use the institutions of the Union to develop "closer cooperation" between themselves in a particular area of Third Pillar activity. The authorizing decision is to be taken by qualified majority in the Council but it will be possible, in the last resort, for a Member State which is opposed, to block a decision.

Asylum

3.22   A Protocol on asylum to be attached to the EC Treaty will set out the conditions under which an application for asylum by a citizen of a Member State may be considered by any other Member State. However, it will not affect the legal obligation on Member States under the 1951 Convention on the Status of Refugees, and the 1967 Protocol, to consider each asylum application individually.

Employment

3.23   During the negotiations, Member States recognised that much needs to be done at national or at business level to stimulate employment but that there is considerable scope for coordination by Member States on employment issues and for supporting action by the Community. To help to achieve this a set of new procedures will be added to the EC Treaty as a separate Title. These will aim at producing a coordinated Community strategy on employment, which will take account also of the coordination of economic policy which already takes place within the Community.

3.24   Under these procedures, the European Council will adopt conclusions each year on the basis of a joint report from the Council and the Commission. The Council, drawing on these conclusions, will then set guidelines for the employment policies of Member States. Each Member State is to report annually. The Council will monitor compliance with the guidelines; it may make recommendations to Member States and adopt incentive measures. There will also be a new Employment Committee (with two members from each Member State and from the Commission) which could help to provide greater coherence between economic and employment policies in the Community.

Social Policy

3.25   The "schism" which developed in the Community over Social Policy in the early 1990s when the UK refused to accept the Social Chapter has been healed. The terms of the Social Agreement, which, in accordance with the provisions of the Maastricht Social Protocol, were applied by 14 Member States only (including Ireland) but not by the UK, will be brought into the EC Treaty and strengthened to some extent. They will now be applied by all fifteen Member States as part of the EC Treaty.

Social exclusion

3.26 A legal basis for action by the Council to deal with social exclusion through incentive measures will now be included in the EC Treaty. The agreement to do this arose from a proposal made and pressed by Ireland during the negotiation of the new Treaty.

Environment

3.27 The environment provisions of the EC Treaty will be strengthened in certain ways and the concept of *"balanced and sustainable development"* approved at the World Environment and Development Summit in Rio in 1992 will be highlighted. The "integration principle" which requires that environmental considerations be taken into account in all other policies, has been brought up to the front of the Treaty.

3.28 Under the present EC Treaty a Member State, subject to Commission approval, may retain its own stricter environmental measures even after a Community harmonisation measure has been adopted by the Council. This provision will be retained and extended to measures adopted by the Commission. In addition, a new provision will be added which will permit a Member State, subject to Commission approval, to introduce new stricter national measures if it can produce scientific evidence of a problem which arose for it after the Community harmonisation measure was adopted. If the Commission allows a national measure to be introduced in such a case, then it will be required to consider whether similar measures should be applied throughout the Union.

Public Health

3.29 The new Treaty will add provisions to the EC Treaty which will allow the Community to set safety standards for human organs and blood and blood derivatives and also permit it to take public health measures to protect against animal and plant diseases. But fundamental responsibility for health services and medical care will remain at Member State level and the Treaty will recognise this.

Consumer protection

3.30 The provisions in the EC Treaty on consumer protection issues are to be strengthened through a greater focus on consumer rights including the right to information. There will now be a specific requirement to take consumer protection concerns into account in implementing all other Community policies and activities.

Subsidiarity

3.31   Subsidiarity means essentially doing things at the lowest level at which they can be done effectively. So in areas where it shares competence with Member States (that is in areas not within its exclusive competence) the Community should act only if there is real "added value" by comparison with action by Member States only. But subsidiarity is a dynamic concept — it allows action by the Community to be expanded where it is justified and, conversely, to be restricted where this is no longer the case.

3.32   The Maastricht Treaty of 1992 wrote the principle of subsidiarity into the EC Treaty (Article 3b) and this formulation will not be changed. However, there is a detailed new Protocol which draws largely, with some adaptations, on the rules about implementation of the principle which all Member States agreed to in 1992 in the conclusions of the European Councils of Edinburgh and Birmingham. These provisions, accepted by all since 1992 as a political commitment, will now have full legal force as a Protocol to the EC Treaty.

Transparency and access to EC documents

3.33   New provisions are to be added to the EC Treaty to ensure greater openness and a right of access to EC documents, subject to general rules to be set by the Council and detailed rules for implementation by each institution.

Right to correspond in Irish

3.34   A new provision added to the EC Treaty will mean that any Union citizen may write to any of the Community institutions or bodies in one of the twelve Treaty languages and expect that any reply received will be in the same language. Irish is a Treaty language (although not an official or a working language). Thus, an Irish person, or any other EU citizen, who wishes to correspond in Irish with the EC institutions and bodies may do so.

Common Foreign and Security Policy (CFSP)

3.35   The CFSP (Second Pillar) provisions of the EU (Maastricht) Treaty of 1992 will be re-structured and developed with a view to making the foreign and security policy role of the Union more effective and more coherent.

3.36   The decision-making procedures in particular are to be recast in a way intended to make them work to better effect. An innovation is that the European Council may adopt *"common strategies"* in particular areas or aspects of foreign policy on the recommendation of the Council. Such decisions, like all decisions of the European Council, would be taken by unanimity. Once this is done, and for as long as the common strategy applies, voting in the Council on subsequent measures in those areas will in principle be by qualified majority. However, an "emergency brake" procedure will allow any Member State to block a decision *"for important and stated reasons of national policy"* — although if a sufficient number of other Member States insist, the issue may be submitted to the European Council for decision by unanimity. Thus, if the Member State which is opposed maintains its position it can block a decision.

3.37   There will also be a new provision for *"constructive abstention"* which will allow a Member State to let a decision be adopted as a decision committing the Union while itself "opting out" of any obligation to apply it.

3.38   The new Treaty will provide that operational expenditure will be charged to the Community budget except for expenditure arising from operations having security and defence implications and cases where the Council unanimously decides otherwise.

3.39   The Secretary General of the Council will now be *"High Representative for the Common Foreign and Security Policy"*. In that capacity he/she will assist the Council by contributing to the formulation and implementation of policy. At the request of the Presidency, the Secretary General as "High Representative" will also be able to conduct political dialogue on behalf of the Council with other countries and organisations.

Security/Defence aspect of the CFSP

3.40   The new Treaty will also make changes to the Article of the Maastricht Treaty (Article J.4) which extended the CFSP to all questions related to the security of the Union. These changes are explained further in the following paragraphs.

Scope of the CFSP in the defence area

3.41   The Maastricht Treaty of 1992 already says that the Common Foreign and Security Policy (CFSP) *"shall include all questions related to the security of the Union, including the eventual framing of a common defence policy which might in time lead to a common defence"*. The new text will provide that the CFSP *"shall include all questions relating to the security of the Union, including the progressive framing of a common defence policy in accordance with the second sub-paragraph, which might lead to a common defence should the European Council so decide. It shall in that case recommend to the Member States the adoption of such a decision in accordance with their respective constitutional requirements"*

3.42   The *"second sub-paragraph"* referred to deals with the role of the WEU (Western European Union). It provides in particular that the WEU *"supports the*

Union in framing the defence aspects of the Common Foreign and Security Policy as set out in this Article."

3.43   In the new formulation, the concept of a future common defence continues to be referred to in the language of possibility (*"might"*). Any decision about it would be taken by the European Council, that is to say at Summit level where all decisions are by unanimity; and it would then be referred as a recommendation to each of the Member States for adoption in accordance with its respective constitutional requirements. The Irish Government, like the two previous Governments, have stated that, whether or not such a decision would require an amendment of the Constitution, it would be put to the people for decision in a referendum.

EU/WEU relations and Petersberg Tasks

3.44   The Maastricht Treaty already refers to the WEU as *"an integral part of the development of the Union"*; and it provides that the EU is to request the WEU to carry out EU decisions which have defence implications. The new Treaty repeats that the WEU is *"an integral part of the development of the Union"*. It adds that the WEU provides the Union *"with access to an operational capability notably in the context of paragraph 2"*. This is a reference to the Petersberg tasks — see below. As in the earlier Treaty the EU will continue to use the WEU to *"elaborate and implement"* any of its decisions which have defence implications. The Treaty will provide, however, that decisions of this kind are to be taken *"without prejudice to the policies and obligations referred to in paragraph 1, third sub-paragraph"*. (This is a reference to the safeguard provision in relation to Ireland's position, which is explained in paragraphs 3.48 and 3.49 below).

3.45   For these reasons, the Union is to *"foster closer institutional relations with the WEU with a view to the possibility of the integration of the WEU into the Union, should the European Council so decide."* If the European Council were to take such a decision, then it would recommend it for adoption to the Member States *"in accordance with their respective constitutional requirements"*.

3.46   The language here is similar to that used above about the possibility of a common defence. In either case the decision would first have to be adopted by unanimity at Summit level in the European Council and then recommended to the Member States for adoption in accordance with their respective constitutional requirements (see also paragraph 3.43 above.)

Petersberg Tasks

3.47   The new Treaty text provides that questions under the Article are to include humanitarian and rescue tasks, peacekeeping tasks and tasks of combat forces in crisis management including peacemaking. These are commonly called "the Petersberg tasks". If, in a particular case, the Union were to decide on one of these tasks, it would avail itself of the WEU to carry it out. All Member States of the Union would be entitled to take part, but there would be no obligation on any Member State to do so. Any Member State which participated in the tasks in question would be able to play a full and equal part in planning and decision-taking in the WEU.

Other provisions

3.48 The new Treaty text will repeat a sentence in the existing Maastricht Treaty which, as well as requiring Union policy to respect the obligations of those States which are members of NATO, also provides that *"the policy of the Union in accordance with this Article shall not prejudice the specific character of the security and defence policy of certain Member States."*

3.49 When it was originally included in the Maastricht Treaty this was intended as a provision which would safeguard the special position of Ireland in relation to military or defence involvement. Since the reference is indirect and general it may now also be read as covering the particular positions of those other Member States who are not members of alliances.

3.50 The new Treaty will also add a provision which will allow any Member States which so wish to cooperate in the matter of armaments.

3.51 The Treaty will also add to the EU Treaty a clause providing for a future review of the provision of this Article dealing with security aspects of the CFSP. This would make it necessary to call another Intergovernmental Conference to discuss possible revisions to the Treaty. Any changes would require unanimity of all Member States for adoption and amendments to the Treaty would come into effect only if ratified by each Member State. However, no date or time frame has been set for such a review.

External Economic Relations

3.52 The EC Treaty at present prescribes the procedure to be followed when the Community engages in international trade negotiations. The Commission, acting within a mandate from the Council, conducts the negotiations, with help and advice from a committee comprising representatives of the Member States. The Council concludes the negotiations, which means that individual ratification of the outcome by each Member State is not necessary. Decisions of the Council are to be taken in many cases by qualified majority vote.

3.53 However, these procedures apply in the main only to negotiations about trade in goods. They do not, by and large, cover negotiations on services and on intellectual property rights, areas which have become of great importance internationally in recent years

3.54   At the conclusion of the negotiations on the new Treaty, it was agreed to include a provision in the EC Treaty which will, in effect, allow the Council to decide by unanimity at a future date, to extend these procedures to issues relating to services and to intellectual property.

Protocol on Institutions

3.55   A Protocol is to be attached to the EU Treaty and the three Community Treaties to deal with the linked issues of the future size of the Commission and the possible re-weighting of votes in the Council. It can be summarised as follows:

(a) There will be no change in the size of the Commission or in the weighting of votes in the Council until the next enlargement of the Union;

(b) As from the entry of the first new Member States to the Union, the larger Member States (France, Germany, Italy, Spain and the UK) will give up their second Commissioner and each Member State for the future will nominate just one Commissioner — on condition that, by then, a solution which compensates the larger Member States but which is acceptable to all, has been found for the issue of the weighting of votes in the Council. This could be either a revision of voting weights or a "dual majority" requirement. The Commission would then have fifteen members plus one additional member for each new Member State admitted.

(c) One year before the membership of the EU is due to exceed twenty another Intergovernmental Conference will be called to undertake a comprehensive review of the institutions of the Union.

3.56   Thus, in practice:

(i) there is no change in the right of each Member State to nominate a full member of the Commission;

(ii) at some time between now and the date when the first of the new Members join the Union, there will be a further negotiation on the re-weighting of Council votes (with a view to compensating the five largest Member States for giving up their right to nominate a second Commissioner). On the assumption that this is successful the membership of the Commission will be one per Member State;

(iii) there will be a major review of institutions at another IGC which is to be called a year before the sixth new Member is due to join;

(iv) nothing has been done to prejudge the outcome of that review.

(v) there is an assumption in this sequence of events that the first group of new Member States admitted together will number five or less. If it should exceed five, then an IGC would be triggered one year before they are admitted.

Extension of QMV

3.57   The new Treaty will bring about some extension of the areas where decisions in the Council on matters under the First Pillar are to be taken by qualified majority vote. It will also provide for qualified majority voting on certain kinds of decisions under the Second Pillar (CFSP) — subject, however, to the ultimate right of a Member State to apply an "emergency brake" to block a decision. Under the Third Pillar implementation of binding decisions, agreed by unanimity, will be by qualified majority.

3.58   The authorisation to a group of Member States to avail of the institutions of the Union for "closer cooperation" between themselves ("flexibility") under the First and the Third Pillars, will also be granted by the Council by a qualified majority vote but this too is subject to the ultimate right of a Member State to apply the "emergency brake" to block a decision.

Role of the European Parliament

3.59   The new Treaty will impose an upper limit of 700 on the membership of the Parliament, which is now 626. It will also strengthen the role of the Parliament through a fairly considerable extension of the scope of the "co-decision procedure". The procedure itself will also be simplified somewhat. The co-decision procedure makes the Parliament in effect a co-legislator with the Council in the adoption of Community legislation. In its final stages the agreement of both institutions is necessary for the adoption of Community legislation.

Role of National Parliaments

3.60   A Protocol to be added to all four Treaties will provide for a better flow of information to National Parliaments and will recognise a certain role for COSAC (the Conference of European Affairs Committees).

Role of the President of the Commission

3.61   The role of the President will be strengthened in certain ways, so that he/she will have greater political authority within the "College" of the Commission. At present the Member States nominate the President of the Commission "by common accord" after consulting the European Parliament and they then nominate the other Members of the Commission "in consultation with" the nominee for President. Under the new Treaty the nomination by the Member States of a person to be President will first be submitted for approval to the Parliament. Once the Parliament has approved the nomination, the Member States will nominate the other Members of the Commission "by common accord" with the nominee for President. In a Declaration the Member States also express the view that the President must enjoy broad discretion in the allocation of tasks within the Commission as well as in any re-shuffling of those tasks during the term of office of a Commission.

Other institutional issues

3.62   There will be some extension of the jurisdiction of the Court of Justice and some strengthening of the position of the Court of Auditors as well as of the positions of the Economic and Social Committee and the Committee of the Regions. There will be stronger provisions on the fight against fraud affecting the financial interests of the Community; and a new legal basis in the EC Treaty for collection and production of statistics. A Protocol to be added to all four Treaties will confirm existing arrangements for the location of the institutions.

"Closer cooperation" ("Flexibility")

3.63   The new Treaty will add general provisions to the EU and the EC Treaties which will allow a group of Member States less than the full membership but constituting at least a majority to use the EU institutions to develop "closer cooperation" between themselves under the First (Community) and the Third (Police and Judicial Cooperation in Criminal matters) Pillars. These provisions will not, however, apply to the two other Community Treaties (Coal and Steel and Euratom). Authorisation is to be granted by qualified majority vote of the Council but there is an "emergency brake" procedure which will allow a Member State, in the last resort to block a decision. No similar provision for flexibility will apply under the Second Pillar (CFSP), since the new "constructive abstention" procedure makes it unnecessary.

3.64   Certain areas will be excluded completely and, in addition, some detailed conditions to be complied with are set. This could have the effect of limiting the extent to which the new provisions will actually be used in practice.

Simplification and re-numbering of the Treaties

3.65   There are many articles and provisions in the existing Treaties which make up the structure of the Union which have become obsolete over time for one reason or another. Obsolete articles are now being deleted from the Treaties establising the three Communities and the new Treaty will make the necessary legal dispositions for this.

3.66   The opportunity is also being taken to renumber the articles of the EU Treaty and the EC Treaty (but not of the other Community Treaties). What is described as a "consolidated version" of both Treaties has been prepared. This shows the two Treaties as they will be when (a) the various additions, deletions and amendments provided for in the new Treaty of Amsterdam have been made; (b) obsolete articles have been deleted; and (c) all articles in each of the two Treaties have been re-numbered in numerical sequence.

3.67   This "consolidated version" will obviously provide a very useful point of reference for the future in consulting the Treaties. However, from a strictly legal viewpoint, it is not this document but the Treaty as signed, showing all the detail of the amendments, which will have full legal status.

Section III

A Detailed Account of the Treaty

CHAPTER FOUR

Fundamental rights and non-discrimination

Fundamental rights

Background — the present position

4.1   All Member States of the European Union are democracies, committed to respect human rights and fundamental freedoms; and as members of a wider organisation, the Council of Europe, all Member States of the European Union are parties to the European Convention on Human Rights.

4.2   The Maastricht Treaty takes this Council of Europe Convention as a standard for human rights for the European Union. Article F.2 of the Treaty imposes an obligation on the Union to *"respect fundamental rights as guaranteed by the European Convention for the Protection of Human Rights and Fundamental Freedoms signed in Rome on 4 November 1980 and as they result from the constitutional traditions common to the Member States as general principles of Community law"*.

4.3   The Court of Justice does not have explicit jurisdiction at present to enforce this provision. Nevertheless, in its jurisprudence, the Court has made it clear that it sees respect for fundamental rights as one of the general principles of Community law which it has a duty to apply in cases which come before it. Indeed it has said that it is a condition for the lawfulness of Community acts that they conform to human rights standards.

4.4   During the negotiation of the new Treaty there was general agreement that the time had come to strengthen these provisions and to make them more explicit in the Treaty so that it would be clear that a commitment to democracy and to respect for human rights is fundamental to membership of the Union.

4.5   Some Member States wanted to go further by having the Union or the Communities as such adhere to the European Convention on Human Rights. This was not agreed since other Member States believed that it could cause serious legal difficulties and lead to a conflict of jurisdictions between the European Court of Human Rights in Strasbourg and the Communities' own Court of Justice in Luxembourg.

What the new Treaty will do

4.6   It was agreed in the new Treaty of Amsterdam, however, to strengthen the existing Treaty commitments in a number of ways and to affirm explicitly that the identity of the Union is based on democracy and human rights. The new Treaty will do this in four main ways.

4.7   **First,** it adds to the European Union Treaty an explicit statement that *"the Union is founded on the principles of liberty, democracy, respect for human rights and fundamental freedoms and the rule of law, principles which are common to the Member States."* (Article F).

4.8   **Second**, it makes respect for these principles a condition which other European States which wish to apply for membership of the Union must meet (Article O).

4.9   **Third,** it establishes, for the first time, a sanctions provision which can be applied to a Member State which turns its back in a fundamental way on these principles.

4.10   The procedure involved is a heavy one, to be invoked in special circumstances only. It requires a proposal by one third of the Member States or by the Commission and the assent of the European Parliament, acting by a two thirds majority vote, representing a majority of its members. In such a case, the Council, meeting at Head of State or Government level, may, by unanimity, *"determine the existence of a serious and persistent breach"* of these principles by a Member State, after hearing the views of the State concerned.

4.11   Once this is done, the Council at the ordinary level, may decide by a qualified majority to suspend certain rights of the Member State under the Treaties including the voting rights of its representative in the Council. Later, if the situation changes, the Council may decide also by qualified majority, to vary or revoke these sanctions (A new Article (F1) containing these provisions is to be added to the EU Treaty and corresponding Articles inserted in the three Community Treaties).

4.12   **Fourth,** in those areas of the First and Third Pillars where it has jurisdiction, the Court of Justice will now explicitly be given power to ensure that actions by the institutions of the Union respect fundamental rights. Article F.2 of the EU Treaty already imposed an obligation on the Union to respect such rights (see paragraph 4.2 above). In any area where it has jurisdiction the Court will now have power to enforce it (Article L (d)).

4.13   As a further step in the protection of rights, the new Treaty provides that Community acts which protect individuals in relation to processing of personal data will apply to Community institutions and bodies as from January 1999. The Council is to establish an independent supervisory body to monitor compliance and it may adopt other provisions as appropriate (Article 213b of the EC Treaty).

Non-discrimination

Background — the present position

4.14   There are already several provisions in the EC Treaty in relation to discrimination. Discrimination on grounds of nationality between citizens of Member States is prohibited. The Treaty also provides that each Member State shall apply the principle of equal pay for equal work to men and women. These provisions have been further developed and added to over a number of years by secondary legislation and by decisions of the Court of Justice.

What the new Treaty will do

4.15   The new Treaty will develop and further extend the provisions on equality between men and women; and it will provides for action by the Council to combat discrimination in a wide range of other areas. The changes are explained further below.

Equality between men and women

4.16   Existing Community law on equality between the sexes relates to equal pay for equal work and other matters related to the workplace. The new Treaty extends this obligation beyond the workplace. A general obligation will now be imposed on the Community in all its activities to aim to eliminate inequalities and to promote equality, between men and women (Article 3.2 of EC Treaty).

4.17   Furthermore, the provisions of the Social Agreement signed at Maastricht will now be brought into the EC Treaty. This means that its detailed provisions in relation to equal pay for equal work which, like the rest of the Social Agreement, applied until now to fourteen Member States only, will apply to all fifteen (see also section on Social Policy in Chapter 11 below).

4.18   These provisions oblige each Member State to ensure that the principle of equal pay for equal work or work of equal value is applied; and they require the Council, acting in co-decision with the European Parliament, and after consulting the Economic and Social Committee, to adopt measures to ensure its application. They also set out clearly what is meant by terms such as "pay" and "equal pay without discrimination based on sex"; and they allow for positive action to redress existing imbalances. A Declaration by the Member States stipulates that such action should in the first instance aim at improving the situation of women in working life.

Action against discrimination on other grounds

4.19   The new Treaty will add an article to the EC Treaty (Article 6a) which will allow the Council to take action in regard to discrimination in a range of other areas. The Council is to act unanimously, on a proposal by the Commission and after consulting the European Parliament. Following this procedure, and within the limits of its powers, it may take appropriate action to combat discrimination based on sex, racial or ethnic origin, religion or belief, disability, age or sexual orientation.

Declarations

4.20   A number of declarations bearing on aspects of rights have also been made by the Member States in adopting the new Treaty. Such Declarations express the intentions of the Member States and they have political rather than legal force. They cover the following issues:

Persons with a disability
In drawing up measures in relation to the internal market, the Community institutions are to take account of the needs of persons with a disability.

Status of churches and philosophical and non-confessional organisations
The Union will respect the status of such bodies under national law in the Member States.

Abolition of the death penalty
The Declaration notes that since the signature in 1983 of a Protocol to the European Convention on Human Rights the death penalty has not been applied in any Member State and has been abolished in most. The Protocol has been signed and ratified by a large majority of EU Member States. On the face of it this Declaration does no more than note the situation which actually obtains in the Union. However, in context, it carries a certain political weight as a pointer towards the idea that the death penalty should not apply in Member States.

CHAPTER FIVE

An area of freedom, security and justice

5.1 The new Treaty sets as an objective the establishment of the Union, by progressive stages, as an area of freedom, security and justice.

5.2 This will be done in part through the strengthened provisions on fundamental rights and new measures to combat discrimination which were explained in Chapter 4 above. These will affirm that the Union is founded on the principles of liberty, democracy, respect for human rights and fundamental freedoms and the rule of law; there will be a new sanctions provision which may be invoked if a Member State is in serious and persistent breach of these principles; and it will be made clear that only States which respect them may be admitted as new Members.

5.3 Along with these provisions touching on freedom and liberty which were explained in Chapter 4, the new Treaty will also contain detailed new provisions on freedom of movement for persons within the Union. It will also have new provisions on security of persons and on justice issues — the two other aspects of the overall aim which the Union has set for itself.

5.4 These provisions are both extensive and complex. They will be dealt with in detail in Chapters 6 to 10 below. The aim of the present chapter is to explain the background and the issues which had to be addressed; and to give a general outline of how the various inter-linked provisions intended to achieve the overall objective will fit into the general structure of the Treaties.

Background

The principle of freedom of movement

5.5 The free movement of persons is already established as one of the fundamental objectives of the EC Treaty. Article 7a provides that:

> *"The internal market shall comprise an area without internal frontiers in which the free movement of goods, persons, services and capital is ensured in accordance with the provisions of this Treaty."*

5.6   The counterpart to freedom of movement within the Union has to be close cooperation and coordinated action on entry to the Union across its external borders; and close cooperation between Member States in preventing and combating crime. Otherwise Member States will be reluctant to lift their national frontier controls.

Border controls

5.7   These general aims are shared by all Member States. But there has been some disagreement between them which focused in part on whether "persons" should be understood to mean only citizens of the Union or all persons legally within its frontiers. Continental Member States generally take the latter view. They have accepted the aim of removing all checks and controls at their common borders (which are often referred to as the "internal borders" of the Union). The UK on the other hand has always insisted on its right to maintain checks and controls at its ports of entry, while accepting that, after suitable identity checks, free entry must be allowed to those who establish that they are citizens of Member States of the Union or of Iceland, Norway or Liechtenstein which are members of the European Economic Area. Ireland's concern is to maintain the Common Travel Area between it and the UK (see paragraph 5.11 below).

Schengen cooperation

5.8   Because of this disagreement, it has not proved possible so far, by action within the Treaties, to make the Union an area without internal frontier controls. Instead, since 1985, a number of Member States have committed themselves through a separate framework of intergovernmental cooperation which they have developed between themselves outside the Treaties — the so-called Schengen Agreements — to lift controls at their mutual frontiers.

5.9   Schengen is the name of the town where the agreements were signed. It has come to be used loosely as a convenient way to describe the agreements (1985 and 1990) and the cooperation which has developed under their terms.

5.10   Schengen cooperation as it has developed over more than a decade involves a commitment by the States taking part to free movement of persons, without border controls, across their common borders, coupled with close cooperation between the countries concerned on related issues — particularly justice issues and issues related to entry to the Schengen area from other countries outside it. This system, which began with five countries participating now involves thirteen Member States of the Union as members or prospective members, as well as Norway and Iceland which signed an agreement to become associated with it in December 1996.

Position of Ireland

5.11   Ireland, like Continental Member States, understands *"free movement of persons"* in the EC Treaty to mean in principle all persons of whatever nationality, who are legally within the European Union. But Ireland shares a Common Travel Area with the UK and it wants to maintain for citizens of both countries the benefits of freedom of travel between the two jurisdictions, without passport or visa, which that allows. It makes sense to do so since more than 70% of travel to and from Ireland goes to, or through, UK jurisdiction. The fact that Ireland has not joined the Schengen Agreements or committed itself to the complete lifting of frontier controls with other Member States which they envisaged reflects its wish to maintain the Common Travel Area.

Bringing Schengen within the Treaties

5.12   Schengen cooperation has grown and developed in many respects outside the Treaties but the thirteen EU Member States who participate in it now want to see it brought within the framework of the Treaties. They believe that this would make it more open and more democratically accountable and would help to ensure better protection of individual rights. It was eventually agreed to do this in the new Treaty, as described in Chapter 9 below, subject to special provision for the particular positions of Ireland, the UK and Denmark and for Norway and Iceland.

Outline summary of what the new Treaty will do

5.13   This is the general background against which negotiations took place at the Intergovernmental Conference. The new Treaty which was the outcome of those negotiations seeks to address the issues through a series of inter-related steps which will amend the EC Treaty (First Pillar) and the EU Treaty (Third Pillar) and add new provisions and Protocols to both. These steps are summarised in the following paragraphs of this Chapter. They will be explained in more detail in the immediately succeeding Chapters of this White Paper.

I. Objective

5.14   **First,** the new Treaty will fix an overall aim by adding a new objective to Article B of the EU Treaty where the objectives of the European Union are set out:

> *"to maintain and develop the Union as an area of freedom, security and justice, in which the free movement of persons is assured in conjunction with appropriate measures with respect to external border controls, asylum, immigration, and the prevention and combating of crime."*

II. New Title on free movement, immigration and related issues

5.15   **Second,** the new Treaty will insert into the EC Treaty (the First Pillar) a new Title IIIa comprising nine Articles. This will give the Community as such competence to adopt measures relating to free movement of persons within the Union, visas, asylum, immigration, refugees, judicial cooperation in civil matters and related issues; and it will set out a five year programme for the Community to follow in doing so. This new Title is explained in more detail in Chapter 6 below.

III. Protocols allowing exemptions

5.16   **Third,** the new Treaty will also add to the EC and EU Treaties three new Protocols bearing on this new Title which is now to be inserted into the EC Treaty. These Protocols (which are explained in more detail in Chapter 7 below) are necessary to provide for the particular positions of the UK, Ireland and Denmark respectively.

5.17   One of these Protocols will exempt the UK from the terms of Article 7a of the EC Treaty which could otherwise require it to abolish all controls at points of entry from other Member States. It will also exempt Ireland for so long as the Common Travel Area arrangements exist between Ireland and the UK; and it will, for the first time, give formal recognition to the Common Travel Area.

5.18   A separate Protocol will exempt Ireland and the UK specifically from the provisions of the new Title on freedom of movement, immigration etc. It will however, allow either country, or both, on certain conditions, to opt in to a proposal before it is adopted or to join in applying a measure after it is adopted. Ireland may also at any stage indicate that it wants to end its exemption entirely and be bound by the new Title.

5.19   Another Protocol relates only to Denmark. It will exempt Denmark from participating in measures under the new Title except for some relating to visas; and it will allow it, under certain conditions, to make its own decisions about whether or not to implement Council decisions taken under the new Title with a view to building on existing Schengen arrangements.

IV. Re-structuring of the Third Pillar (Justice and Home Affairs)

5.20   **Fourth,** the new Treaty will lead to a substantial revision of the provisions of the EU Treaty in the area of Justice and Home Affairs — the so-called "Third Pillar" of the Union. The intention is to strengthen and re-organise police and judicial cooperation within the Union on criminal matters wherever there are cross-border aspects. The list of crimes to be dealt with will be revised and extended; decision-making will be improved; and there will be a greater role for the Court of Justice. These provisions are explained in detail in Chapter 8 below.

V. Protocol integrating Schengen into the Treaties

5.21 **Fifth,** the new Treaty will bring the whole Schengen arrangement and what it has achieved to date into the framework of the Treaties. Under a special Protocol, which is to be annexed to both the EU and the EC Treaties, decisions already taken in Schengen will apply to thirteen EU Member States and may be built on further. Ireland and the UK, on certain conditions, will be able to opt in to all or part of these decisions, taken initially outside the Treaties but now brought within them; and will be able to join, if they so wish, in building on them. A special agreement will be negotiated to associate Iceland and Norway with these arrangements. This Schengen Protocol is explained in greater detail in Chapter 9 below.

VI. Protocol on asylum

5.22 **Sixth,** a Protocol will set out the conditions under which a Member State may consider an application for asylum by a national of another EU State. It will not, however, affect the obligations of Member States under the 1951 Convention on the Status of Refugees. This Protocol is explained in detail in Chapter 10 below.

5.23 These six inter-related provisions, taken together, are an approach by the new Treaty towards developing the Union as an area of freedom, security and justice. They envisage steps towards complete freedom of movement of persons within the Union being taken in conjunction with decisions to implement appropriate "flanking measures" and subject to the exemptions and opt outs which the various Protocols allow to the UK, to Ireland and to Denmark. Chapters 6 to 10 will deal in turn with the detail of what the Treaty will do in each of these six areas.

CHAPTER SIX

New Treaty Title on free movement of persons, immigration and related issues

6.1   The Treaty of Amsterdam will add to the EC Treaty a new Title III (a) with nine Articles covering visas, asylum, immigration and other policies related to free movement of persons. This will set a five year programme of work for the Council. The present Chapter explains these provisions in greater detail.

What the new Treaty will do

6.2   The new Title will not itself have the effect of bringing the measures which will be necessary into force. What it will do is rather spell out in some detail the areas in which measures are to be taken by the Council over the five year period; what those measures are to cover; and by what procedure and in what time frame they are to be adopted.

Outline of five year work programme

6.3   The <u>first Article</u> (73 i) sets out this programme of work in summary form. Within five years of entry into force of the Treaty, the Council is to adopt measures aimed at ensuring the free movement of persons within the Union without frontier controls, in conjunction with directly related "flanking measures".

6.4   The "flanking measures" will be of two kinds:

(i) those relating to external border controls, asylum and immigration and other related areas which will fall under the new Title and which when they are adopted will form part of Community law. (These are explained in the present Chapter)

(ii) other measures to prevent and combat crime which will be undertaken as part of the inter-governmental cooperation in the fields of Justice and Home Affairs — the so-called "Third Pillar" established by the Maastricht Treaty, which will be re-named as *"Provisions on Police and Judicial Cooperation in Criminal Matters"* (as explained in Chapter 8 below).

Border controls

6.5   A <u>second Article</u>   (73 j) deals directly with the issue of border controls. Within five years of the entry into force of the new Treaty, the Council is required to adopt measures in relation to three issues:

(1) **Internal borders**: the measures are to ensure that there are no controls on any persons crossing the borders between Member States within the Union;

(2) **External borders:** the measures will establish

(a) standards and procedures for border checks on persons crossing the external borders of the Union; and

(b) rules on the granting of visas for stays of up to three months, (including such matters as an agreed list of countries whose nationals will require visas and a common format for visas);

(3) The conditions under which **nationals of countries outside the Union** may travel freely within the Union for up to three months.

Protocol on agreements with other countries

6.6   A <u>Protocol</u> to be added to the EC Treaty will allow Member States to conclude agreements with other countries outside the Union so long as they respect Community law and other relevant international agreements (This provision was requested by Finland which has a long common border with Russia).

Declaration on foreign policy considerations in granting visas

6.7   A <u>Declaration</u> made by the Member States accepts that foreign policy considerations are to be taken into account when measures on visas are being adopted by the Council. (This was requested by Portugal which has particular arrangements with former colonies).

Immigration policy, asylum and refugees

6.8   The <u>third Article</u> in the new Title (73 k) deals with asylum, refugees and immigration policy. It provides that the Council is to adopt measures on:

(1) **asylum:** these measures are to be in accordance with the 1951 Geneva Convention and the 1967 Protocol on the status of refugees. They will make it clear which Member State is to be responsible for handling an asylum application; and they will establish minimum standards for receiving asylum seekers and for granting or withdrawing refugee status;

43

(2) **refugees and displaced persons**: these measures, which will deal with certain aspects of this issue, will set minimum standards for temporary protection for those who need it; and they will also promote what is described as *"a balance of effort"* — in effect a kind of burden-sharing — between Member States in coping with refugees;

(3) **immigration policy**: these measures will relate to the conditions on which long-term visas and residence permits will be issued by Member States; and they will address the question of illegal immigration, including the repatriation of illegal residents;

(4) **rights of legal residents:** these measures are to define the rights and conditions under which nationals of countries outside the Union who are already legally resident in one Member State may reside in other Member States.

National measures

6.9   The third Article also provides that even after the Council has adopted the measures on (3) immigration policy and (4) rights of legal residence as set out above, Member States will be free to maintain or to introduce their own national measures provided they are compatible with the Treaty and with international agreements. Furthermore, a Declaration states that Member States may reach their own agreements with countries outside the Union about long-term visas and residence permits so long as they respect Community law.

Consultation with UNHCR

6.10   A Declaration by the Member States provides that there is to be consultation with the UN High Commissioner for Refugees and other relevant international organisations on matters relating to asylum policy.

Time frame for decisions

6.11   Most of these measures are to be adopted by the Council within a period of five years after entry into force of the new Treaty. However, measures on burden-sharing, on the conditions for long-term visas and residence and on the rights of legal residents to reside in another Member State are not subject to this time limit.

National responsibility for law and order — emergency situations

6.12   A fourth Article (73 1) provides that the new Treaty provisions do not affect the responsibilities of Member States for law and order and internal security — these remain national responsibilities. It also covers the possibility of an emergency situation where there is a sudden inflow of non-Union nationals into one or more Member States. If that happens, the Council, voting by qualified majority on a Commission proposal, may adopt provisional measures for up to six months.

Judicial cooperation in civil matters

6.13   A <u>fifth Article</u> (73 m) deals with measures on judicial cooperation in civil matters which have cross-border implications. The measures, which are to be taken insofar as they are necessary for the proper functioning of the internal market, include:

   (a) improving and simplifying the system for serving legal documents between the various Member States within the Union; cooperation in taking evidence; and recognition and enforcement of decisions in civil and commercial cases;

   (b) helping to make the rules in Member States on conflict of laws and jurisdictions compatible;

   (c) eliminating obstacles to the good functioning of civil proceedings, if necessary by promoting the compatibility of rules on civil procedure in the different Member States.

Freedom of expression

6.14   A <u>Declaration</u> by the Member States referring to this Article was also adopted at the initiative of Sweden to take account of its constitutional requirements. It states that Member States remain free to apply their own constitutional rules on freedom of the press and freedom of expression in other media.

Cooperation between Administrations

6.15   A <u>sixth Article</u> (73 n) provides that the Council is to take measures to ensure cooperation between Departments in the national administrations of Member States and between those Departments and the Commission in areas covered in the new Title.

Decision-making procedures

6.16   A <u>seventh Article</u> (73 o) dealing with decision-making sets out the procedure to be followed by the Council in adopting measures under the new Title in the various areas set out above. These procedures are explained below.

Possible use of "Community method"

6.17   The new Title will form part of the EC Treaty and it will thus come under the First Pillar. During the negotiation of the new Treaty, however, there was debate about how far to apply the Community procedures and methods of decision-making of the First Pillar to matters which have been dealt with until now under the largely intergovernmental procedures of the Third Pillar. Adopting Community procedures would mean, for example, that the Commission would have the sole right of initiative; there might be areas for qualified majority voting and co-decision with the European Parliament; and the European Court of Justice would exercise jurisdiction.

6.18   The Article as agreed is a compromise. The effect is that for most decisions procedures like those of the Third Pillar will continue to apply for the first five years after the Treaty enters into force. After that period some Community procedures will apply: for example the right of initiative will rest with the Commission. On other matters, however, a decision about how far to go in adopting the Community method will depend on a further unanimous decision to be taken by the Council at that time.

6.19   More specifically, the compromise has three main aspects:

Five year transitional period
   (i)   There will be a five-year transitional period during which the decision-making procedures will be largely similar to those used under the Third Pillar: the right of initiative will be shared between the Commission and the Member States; and the Council will act unanimously after consulting the European Parliament.

After the transitional period
   (ii)   After this 5-year period:

      (a)   the Commission will have the sole right of initiative (it must examine, though not necessarily agree to, any request by a Member State that it make a proposal); and

      (b)   the Council is to decide by unanimity, after consulting the Parliament how far the co-decision procedure used in many areas of the First Pillar (which normally involves qualified majority voting in the Council) should apply to all or part of the new Title. It will also decide about adapting the provisions relating to the powers of the Court of Justice.

Exceptions
   (iii)   There are, however, two exceptions to these provisions:

      (a)   Certain decisions on visas — decisions establishing a list of countries whose nationals will require visas and decisions on a uniform format for visas — are to be dealt with from the outset in accordance with one of the procedures for Community decision-making: they are to be taken by qualified majority vote in the Council, on a proposal by the Commission and after consulting the European Parliament;

(b) After the five year transition period, certain other decisions on visas — those on visa procedures and on the rules for a uniform visa — are to be taken under another of the Community procedures, that of co-decision. This will involve qualified majority voting in the Council and give the European Parliament the role of co-legislator with the Council.

Court of Justice jurisdiction

6.20   An eighth Article (73 p) sets out the role and powers of the Court of Justice in the interpretation of the new Title; and in interpreting and deciding on the validity of acts of the institutions of the Community which are based on it.

(i) Where such a question is raised in a case before a tribunal or court of final appeal in a Member State, that court or tribunal is to ask for a ruling of the Court of Justice if it considers such a ruling necessary to enable it to give judgment in the case;

(ii) The Council, the Commission or any Member State may also ask the Court for a ruling on a question of interpretation of the Title or of acts of the Community institutions based on it. The ruling is not, however, to apply retrospectively to other cases already decided in the courts of Member States;

(iii) The Court will not have jurisdiction to rule on any measure or decision about lifting border controls with other Member States of the Union which relates to law and order and internal security. These areas will continue to be a national responsibility.

Application is subject to the Protocols for Denmark, Ireland and UK

6.21   The ninth Article of the new Title (73 q) provides that the application of the new Title to the UK and Ireland and to Denmark will be subject to the provisions of the respective Protocols in relation to these countries which are now to be annexed to the Treaties. The effects of these Protocols will be explained in greater detail in the next Chapter (Chapter 7).

CHAPTER SEVEN

The Protocols to establish the respective positions of Ireland, the UK and Denmark

7.1   The new Treaty provisions include three Protocols which establish the positions of Ireland and the UK and of Denmark respectively in relation to the issues arising under the new Title on freedom of movement and related matters, which were dealt with in the previous Chapter of this White Paper. These Protocols are to be annexed to both the EU and the EC Treaties. Their effects are explained further below.

(i) Protocol on the position of the UK and of Ireland in relation to the new Title

---

7.2   This Protocol relates specifically to the new Title which has been added to the EC Treaty on free movement, asylum, immigration and judicial cooperation in civil matters. Its effect is to exempt both Ireland and the UK from all of the provisions of the new Title but to permit either or both countries to opt in to particular measures under specified terms and conditions set out in the Protocol.

The reason for a Protocol

7.3   Such a Protocol is necessary primarily because the UK wishes to maintain its controls and checks at ports of entry. It is not willing to participate in measures such as those envisaged in the new Title which would require it to remove all such controls for persons entering from another Member State of the Union. Furthermore, it did not agree that all of these issues should be brought under the First Pillar, which will be the effect of placing the new Title in the EC Treaty.

7.4   Ireland, as explained above, wishes to maintain the Common Travel Area arrangements with the UK. It would not be feasible to do this while at the same time accepting an obligation to lift all controls at ports of entry for persons entering from other Member States of the Union. For this reason, Ireland has joined the UK in availing of the exemptions which the Protocol provides.

What the Protocol will provide

7.5   The first two articles of the Protocol provide that the UK and Ireland shall not take part in the adoption of measures under the new Title on free movement or be bound in any way by them; nor shall such measures form part of Community law for either country.

Right to opt in to a proposal

7.6   Article 3 will, however, allow either Ireland or the UK or both to join in adopting and applying any measure which may be put forward under the Title, subject to giving notice within three months of the date the proposal is presented of a wish to do so. That is to say that either country may opt in before the measure is adopted. However, if, after a reasonable period of time, the proposed measure cannot be adopted with the UK or Ireland taking part, then the other Member States may go ahead with the decision in the Council without their participation. In the event that either country does not take part in the decision, it will not of course be bound by it.

Right to opt in to a measure after it is adopted

7.7   Article 4 establishes a procedure under which either Ireland or the UK may opt in at a later date to a measure which has already been adopted by the Council. In such a case the country concerned notifies the Commission and the Council. The Commission gives its opinion to the Council within three months and the Commission decides within four months whether the request to "opt in" is to be allowed.

Financial costs

7.8   If either Ireland or the UK is not bound by a measure adopted under the new Title, it will not bear any financial costs of the measure except for its normal share of the general administrative costs which may arise for the institutions.

Ireland's right to opt in to the new Title

7.9   Article 8, the final article of the Protocol, is specific to Ireland and its existence distinguishes Ireland's position from that of the UK. This article allows Ireland to give notice at any time that it no longer wishes to be covered by the terms of the Protocol. In that case, the provisions of the new Title will apply to Ireland. In effect therefore Ireland, in addition to the right to opt in

49

on specific measures referred to above, has also a general right to opt in to the new Title at any future time.

(ii) Protocol on the application of the free movement of persons provision of the EC Treaty to the UK and to Ireland

---

7.10   The new Treaty will annex a second Protocol in relation to the UK and Ireland to both the EU and the EC Treaties. This Protocol is directed specifically to Article 7a of the EC Treaty which provides, among other things, for the free movement of persons within the European Union.

7.11   The effect of this Protocol, in summary, will be to allow both the UK and Ireland to maintain their present controls at ports of entry; it will give explicit recognition to the Common Travel Area which has existed for many years between Ireland and the UK; and it will allow both countries to make the arrangements necessary to maintain it. Its provisions are explained in greater detail below.

7.12   The Protocol begins by providing that the UK, notwithstanding the terms of Article 7a of the EC Treaty, or other Treaty provisions or meansures or international agreements concluded by the Community, may exercise controls at its frontiers with other Member States, that is in practice at its ports of entry. These may be such controls as it considers necessary for two purposes:

(a) to verify the entitlement to enter the UK of citizens of other Member States or of countries in the European Economic Area (Iceland, Norway and Liechtenstein) or of other countries whose citizens the UK is bound to admit under an international agreement;

(b) to decide whether or not to admit other persons to the UK.

7.13   The reason for the distinction made between the two categories is that those falling under (a), together with their dependents, have a right to enter either under Community law or under international agreement. The UK will, however, be allowed to maintain the necessary checks to confirm the identity of such persons. Other persons, that is those who come under (b), do not have a similar right to enter. In such cases the UK will itself decide whether or not to permit them to do so.

Common Travel Area

7.14   The Protocol also provides that the UK and Ireland may continue to maintain the Common Travel Area arrangements relating to travel between the two countries while respecting the rights of those entitled to enter their jurisdictions (see previous paragraph). So long as they maintain these arrangements, that is so long as the Common Travel Area continues, Ireland too will have the same exemptions as those allowed to the UK.

Rights of other Member States vis-a-vis Ireland and the UK

7.15   It follows of course that other Member States of the Union in their turn should be entitled to maintain similar controls at their frontiers on persons entering from the UK, or from Ireland so long as the exemptions in the Protocol apply to these two countries. A further provision of the Protocol establishes this.

Distinctive position of Ireland

7.16   The overall effect of the Protocol, as noted above, will be to allow Ireland similar exemptions and the same right to maintain frontier controls as the UK for as long as the Common Travel Area continues. However, the Protocol is so worded as to show that it is needed primarily because the UK wishes to maintain its long-standing controls at ports of entry. The fact that Ireland has obtained the same exemptions can be seen to be due solely to its wish to do what is necessary to maintain the Common Travel Area arrangement between the two countries.

Declaration by Ireland

7.17   This is brought out even more clearly by a Declaration in relation to both Protocols which Ireland has made in signing the new Treaty. In this Declaration Ireland, referring to the first Protocol, states that it intends to exercise its right to opt in on the adoption of measures under the new Title on free movement etc. to the maximum extent compatible with maintenance of the Common Travel Area. As to the second Protocol, Ireland recalls that its participation reflects its wish to maintain the Common Travel Area in order to maximise freedom of movement into and out of Ireland.

Overall effect

7.18   The net effect of all of this in practice is that the UK and Ireland will continue to maintain their present identity checks at points of entry on all persons seeking to enter the Common Travel Area. At the same time they will also continue to meet their obligation, after the necessary identity checks, to allow entry to citizens of other Member States and of Iceland, Norway and Liechtenstein who are entitled under Community law to be admitted. Other Member States will reciprocate — that is they will continue to apply similar identity checks to persons entering from the UK or Ireland while accepting that, subject to such checks, such persons have a right to be admitted.

(iii) Protocol on the position of Denmark

7.19   In addition to the two Protocols relating to the UK and to Ireland, the new Treaty will annex to the EU and the EC Treaties a third Protocol relating to Denmark. Part I of this Protocol deals with Denmark's position in relation to the new Title on free movement, immigration etc.; Part II repeats its position, established since Maastricht, of not participating in decisions under the Common Foreign and Security Policy (Second Pillar) which have defence implications (one of four "opt-outs" in relation to the Maastricht Treaty which were agreed at Edinburgh in 1992); Part III will allow it to decide at any time that it no longer wishes to avail of the Protocol.

7.20   Part I of the Protocol will have the effect of exempting Denmark from involvement in measures under the new Title except for measures establishing a list of countries whose nationals require visas and measures to introduce a uniform visa (Denmark already participates in visa policy decisions, which were transferred to the First Pillar under the Maastricht Treaty).

7.21   During the negotiation of the new Treaty, Denmark took a generally positive view of much of the content of the new Title. However, because of its sensitivity about the political and constitutional issues which might arise for Denmark from any transfer of competence from national to Community level, it was opposed to the incorporation of these provisions into the EC Treaty as part of Community law. Under Part I of the Protocol it will now be exempted from participating in the adoption of measures under the new Title.

7.22   The Protocol also refers to proposals which may be put forward at some point to build further on the provisions and decisions already agreed in Schengen cooperation (the Schengen *acquis*) which are now to be brought within the framework of the Treaties (see Chapter 9).

7.23   Denmark was in the process of joining Schengen when the new Treaty was agreed and proposals which may be made to develop the Schengen *acquis* intergovernmentally under the Third Pillar would seem to present no difficulties in principle for it. However, if these proposals are brought forward under the new Title in the EC Treaty (ie First Pillar) it will not participate in the decisions as explained in paragraph 7.21 above.

7.24   In any such case, Denmark will decide within six months of the adoption of a proposal by the Council (without its participation) whether to implement the proposal in its national law. If it does so, this will create an obligation in international law between it and the Schengen States (as well as Ireland or the UK if those Member States have opted to take part in the particular area of cooperation in question). If it does not so decide, then the Schengen States, including Denmark, will *consider appropriate measures.*

CHAPTER EIGHT

Police and Judicial Cooperation in Criminal Matters (Third Pillar)

8.1   During the negotiations on the new Treaty there was general agreement among the Member States that in establishing the Union as an area of freedom, security and justice it would be necessary to re-structure and strengthen intergovernmental cooperation against crime under the Justice and Home Affairs provisions of the EU (Maastricht) Treaty which constitute the Third Pillar of the Union.

8.2   The new Treaty will do this by making a series of amendments and additions to the EU Treaty and re-naming this whole area of cooperation. This Chapter of the White Paper explains these changes and what they seek to achieve.

Background

8.3   In the mid-1970s, concern about terrorism and international crime led to meetings of the Ministers from Member States responsible for Justice and Home Affairs. Over the following decades a series of <u>ad hoc</u> arrangements developed, mainly within the "European Political Cooperation" framework which had been established initially to coordinate the foreign policy positions of Member States.

The "Third Pillar"

8.4   In 1992 the Treaty on European Union consolidated these diverse arrangements and structured them as the Justice and Home Affairs provisions which form the so-called Third Pillar of the European Union.

8.5   Third Pillar cooperation between the Member States of the Union, like that in the Second Pillar (the Common Foreign and Security Policy) remains largely intergovernmental in character. Commitments and decisions create Treaty obligations for Member States but unlike those arising under the First Pillar they do not become part of Community law.

8.6 Nevertheless, these new frameworks established by the EU Treaty are closely linked to the Community structure of the First Pillar. Although they are diverse in character, all three Pillars, taken together, constitute the European Union. All are served by a single institutional framework: the European Council gives impetus in all areas of the Union; there is a single Council (which may meet in practice in different formations); a single Commission; a single Court of Justice; and a single Parliament.

8.7 As they stand at present the Justice and Home Affairs (Third Pillar) provisions of the EU Treaty start with a commitment by Member States to regard nine areas as "*matters of common interest*". These include asylum and immigration issues; combating drug addiction and international fraud; judicial cooperation in civil and criminal matters; customs cooperation; and police cooperation against terrorism, drugs and other international crime by way of information exchange through Europol.

8.8 Third Pillar decision-making procedures, like those of the Second Pillar, are substantially intergovernmental rather than supra-national in character. In the Third Pillar, three types of legal instrument are provided for at present: joint positions, joint actions and conventions (which require adoption by Member States); the right of initiative on many issues is shared between the Commission and the Member State and remains with the Member States on others; voting is by unanimity — although there is some limited provision for other forms of voting; the role of the Court of Justice in this area is extremely limited; and the role of the European Parliament is not very strong.

8.9 The present Treaty also makes provision for the possibility of transferring some areas of action to the Community framework of the First Pillar by unanimous decision and subject to national ratification but this has not been used to date.

Reasons for change

8.10 A substantial degree of cooperation on Justice and Home Affairs issues has developed between Member States of the Union since the Third Pillar was established by the EU Treaty in 1992 and a good deal has been achieved. Nevertheless during the negotiation of the new Treaty many Member States expressed a concern to see the Treaty provisions in this area adapted and re-structured.

8.11 There was rising concern about drug trafficking, terrorism and the growth of organised crime — much of it operating across international borders. Persons engaged in crime quite often appear sophisticated in their ability to avail of ease of travel and to use modern communications, while law enforcement agencies in their international cooperation often operate with out-moded methods and arrangements. For many Member States it had also become evident that closer cooperation and a more coordinated approach was necessary in immigration policy and in dealing with refugees and asylum-seekers.

8.12   Dissatisfaction with some aspects of the operation of the Third Pillar provisions was also expressed during the negotiations. Some Member States felt that the structures were over-bureaucratic, with too many advisory levels before a decision is taken by the Council. It was also said that there is insufficient Parliamentary accountability within the system; and that there is a need to increase the role of the Court of Justice and to provide better procedures to guarantee fundamental rights. These concerns, expressed frequently during the negotiations, led to agreement that the new Treaty of Amsterdam should make fairly substantial changes to the Justice and Home Affairs provisions of the EU Treaty.

Re-structuring the Third Pillar

8.13   The new Treaty will do this — in part by transferring a range of issues from the EU Treaty (Third Pillar) to constitute the new Title in the EC Treaty to deal with freedom of movement of persons, immigration and related issues (First Pillar); and in part by recasting the provisions of the Third Pillar which will now be grouped under a new heading *"Police and Judicial Cooperation in Criminal Matters"*. The new EC Treaty Title on freedom of movement and related matters and the Protocols referring to it have been described in Chapters 6 and 7 above. The present Chapter will focus on the re-structured provisions of the Third Pillar.

What the new Treaty will do

Objective

8.14   The relevant section of the EU Treaty (Title VI) will now start by stating an objective for the Union:

> *"to provide citizens with a high level of safety within an area of freedom, security and justice by developing common action among the Member States in the fields of police and judicial cooperation in criminal matters and by preventing and combating racism and xenophobia."*

This objective is to be achieved by preventing and combating crime — organised or otherwise — in particular terrorism, trafficking in persons and offences against children, illicit trafficking in drugs and arms, corruption and fraud.

List of types of crime which are to be the subject of cooperation

8.15   Where the Maastricht Treaty listed nine "matters of common interest", the effect of this new provision is to establish a revised and extended list of crimes which the Member States will cooperate in preventing and combating. Among the new elements now included are trafficking in persons, offences against children, and illicit arms trafficking.

Means to achieve objective

8.16   This objective is to be achieved in three ways:

    (i) closer cooperation between police forces, customs and other authorities in Member States. Cooperation will be both direct and through Europol;

    (ii) closer cooperation between judicial and other authorities in Member States;

    (iii) where necessary, approximation of rules on criminal matters in Member States.

8.17   There then follow a series of Articles setting out in detail how this cooperation is to be given effect in practice through common action in order to achieve the objective of a *"high level of safety"* for the citizens of the Union.

Police cooperation

8.18   Police cooperation will take place both directly between the law enforcement agencies in the Member States and through Europol (the European Police Office). Europol itself is to be further developed over a five year period.

8.19   Common action in police cooperation is to include four main areas:

    (i) operational cooperation against crime between the competent authorities including police forces and customs;

    (ii) collection and exchange of information including information on suspicious financial transactions — subject to appropriate data protection rules — in particular through Europol;

    (iii) cooperation and joint initiatives in such areas as training, equipment, exchange of liaison officers and forensic research;

    (iv) common evaluation of investigative techniques relating to serious organised crime.

Europol

8.20   The Council is to promote cooperation through Europol. The Treaty sets out a programme of work identifying particular areas for action over the five years following entry into force of the Treaty. In particular the Council is to:

(a) enable Europol to support and encourage coordinated investigations by the competent authorities in Member States, including operational actions by joint teams in which Europol plays a supporting role;

(b) adopt measures to allow Europol to ask the authorities in Member States to carry out and to coordinate their investigations in specific cases; and also to allow it to develop expertise which will be available to help Member States in investigating organised crime;

(c) promote liaison, in cooperation with Europol, between prosecuting/ investigating officials fighting organised crime ;

(d) set up a research, documentation and statistical network on cross-border crime.

The issue of judicial review

8.21   During the negotiations, many Member States, while concerned to step up police cooperation greatly as part of a concerted effort to deal with serious crime, were concerned also to ensure that such cooperation would remain subject to appropriate judicial review. At the same time, most Member States were unwilling to see this sensitive area of policing become supra-national to the extent that it would if it were to be brought under the jurisdiction of the European Court of Justice.

8.22   For this reason, it was decided to point instead to the need for judicial review by national courts. Accordingly, in a Declaration referring to the new police cooperation provisions, the Member States say that action in the field of police cooperation, including activities of Europol, *"shall be subject to appropriate judicial review"* at national level in each Member State.

Judicial cooperation in criminal matters

8.23   Common action in this area is to include:

(a) improving cooperation between Ministries and judicial authorities in Member States both as to proceedings and the enforcement of decisions;

(b) facilitating extradition between Member States;

(c) ensuring compatibility of rules in Member States insofar as necessary to improve cooperation;

(d) preventing conflicts of jurisdiction between Member States;

(e) in the areas of organised crime, terrorism and drug trafficking progressively adopting measures to establish minimum rules about penalties and about what constitutes crimes.

Declaration on question of minimum penalties

8.24   During the negotiations, some concern was expressed that establishing minimum rules about penalties might seem to involve a new commitment to legislate for minimum sentences for crimes. To meet this concern it was decided to add a Declaration stating that this provision of the new Treaty would not oblige a Member State whose legal system does not provide for minimum sentences to adopt them.

Possible cross-border law-enforcement operations

8.25   The Council is to lay down the conditions and the limitations under which police and law enforcement agencies of one Member State may operate in the territory of another Member State in liaison and in agreement with the authorities of that State.

8.26   This provision means that any action of this kind in the territory of another Member State will become possible only when and if the Council lays down the conditions and the limitations which are to apply. Any such decision of the Council would have to be taken by unanimity (see below). It is clear also from the text that any such operation in another jurisdiction would have to be undertaken in agreement with the competent authorities there and in liaison with them, since it could otherwise be a breach of sovereignty.

National responsibility for law and order

8.27   The new Treaty retains a safeguard provision which was already in the Maastricht Treaty. This stipulates that the Title — which is to say all of the provisions regarding Third Pillar cooperation, including now those of the new Treaty — shall not affect the responsibilities of Member States for law and order and for internal security.

Decision-making

8.28   The new Treaty will amend and re-cast the provisions of the Maastricht Treaty which set out the various kinds of decisions to be taken by the Council in cooperation under the Third Pillar. Member States will still be required as at present to inform and consult one another within the Council with a view to coordinating their action and to establish cooperation between the relevant Departments in their administrations.

8.29   Apart from this there are to be four main kinds of decision, all of which are to be taken by unanimity on the initiative either of the Commission or of a Member State:

(a) **common positions**: will define the approach of the Union to a particular matter;

(b) **framework decisions:** this is a new type of decision in the Third Pillar, modelled on the "Directive" which is used in the Community framework of the First Pillar. It will be used in cases where it is necessary to bring about greater compatibility between the legal provisions in different Member States (this is what is described in the Treaty as *"the approximation of the laws and regulations of Member States"*);

Like an EC Directive, a framework decision will bind the Member States as to the result to be achieved but it will allow each Member State to decide how exactly to legislate for that at national level. The content of a framework decision will not have direct effect. This means that while it will impose an obligation on the Member States to achieve a result by making the necessary changes in its laws, it will not in itself, in the absence of such action at national level, give a ground for a legal action by an individual;

(c) **decisions for other purposes consistent with the objectives of the Treaty** (ie purposes other than the approximation of laws, which will be dealt with under (b) above). Decisions of this kind are to be binding but, like the framework decisions just mentioned, their content will not entail direct effect;

(d) **conventions** which will be recommended to Member States for adoption. This is a type of legal instrument which was already provided for in the Maastricht Treaty (see below).

Conventions

8.30   A convention in the sense referred to here is an international agreement covering specific issues, drafted within the framework of the Third Pillar to achieve one or more of its objectives. The text must first be approved by the Council by unanimity and then recommended to the Member States for adoption in accordance with their particular constitutional requirements. A time limit for Member States to begin this process is to be set by the Council. This does not pre-judge the decision at national level on adoption — it is intended rather to ensure that the procedure will begin within a reasonable time.

8.31   Once a convention has been adopted by at least half of the Member States it will come into effect for those States unless the convention itself says otherwise. A convention cannot come into force for any State until it has been adopted by that State.

Voting — majority required

8.32   Decisions in the Council under any of the above headings are to be made by unanimity with two exceptions. Both of these relate to further decisions by the Council implementing decisions already taken:

(i) measures implementing a decision under (c) above at the level of the Union are to be adopted by qualified majority, requiring at least 62 votes cast by at least 10 Member States. (Qualified majority voting is explained in paragraphs 16.5 and 16.6 below);

(ii) measures implementing a convention [(d) above] are to be adopted in the Council by a majority of two thirds of the States which are parties to the Convention.

Procedural decisions

8.33   It is made explicit that decisions in the Council on procedural matters are to be taken by simple majority as is the case in practice at present.

Publication of decisions

8.34   A Declaration made by the Member States in regard to this section of the Treaty is intended to ensure greater openness. It provides that initiatives (ie proposals) for measures to be adopted, as well as acts actually adopted by the Council, are to be published in the Official Journal.

Jurisdiction of the Court of Justice

8.35   At present, the Court of Justice has no jurisdiction in Third Pillar matters with one possible exception. When drafting a convention the Member States may, if they so wish, include a provision giving the Court jurisdiction to interpret its provisions and to rule on any dispute about its application.

8.36   The new Treaty will extend the role of the Court under the Third Pillar in three respects. It will now have jurisdiction to:

(i) **give preliminary rulings;**

(ii) **review the legality of decisions;**

(iii) **rule on disputes between Member States**.

Each of these provisions on the role of the Court is explained further below.

8.37   The Court will, however, have no jurisdiction to review the validity or the proportionality of operations carried out by the police or other law enforcement agencies of a Member State; or the exercise of a Member State's responsibilities for law and order and internal security.

(i) Preliminary rulings

8.38   Rulings of this kind are already provided for in the EC Treaty (Article 177). Where a point of Community law is raised in a case before a national court that court, before giving judgment, may ask the Court of Justice to rule on the point of Community law. In lower courts this is optional but if the national court is a court of final appeal, it is bound to refer the point raised to the Court of Justice before giving judgment.

8.39   The Third Pillar and the decisions taken under it do not form part of Community law. Nevertheless the new Treaty will extend the authority of the Court of Justice to give preliminary rulings to a wide range of acts adopted under the Third Pillar. The Court will now, on request, give preliminary rulings on:

(a) the validity and interpretation of framework decisions and other decisions [(b) and (c) in paragraph 8.29 above] — that is those decisions of the Council which have binding effect;

(b) the interpretation of conventions;

(c) the validity and interpretation of measures implementing conventions.

Option for individual Member States to accept jurisdiction

8.40   While the jurisdiction of the Court to give preliminary rulings will in principle be extended to these areas, it will remain a matter of choice for each Member State whether or not to accept this extension of jurisdiction.

8.41   A Member State which wishes to do so may make a declaration to that effect at any time. In doing so, it must make a further choice as to whether the right to request such a preliminary ruling will apply (a) only to a court of final appeal or (b) to any of its national courts. A Member State may even go further — according to a Declaration annexed to the Treaty it may reserve the right to provide in its national law that when an issue is raised it will be compulsory for a court of final appeal to refer to the Court of Justice for a preliminary ruling. The declaration, once made, is irrevocable.

8.42   A number of Member States, including Ireland, have not as yet made such a declaration. However, on the occasion of the signing of the Treaty of Amsterdam on 2 October 1997 five Member States — Austria, Belgium, Germany, Greece and Luxembourg — made declarations and accepted option (b). Four of these — Austria, Belgium, Germany and Luxembourg — further reserved the right to provide in national law that a court of final appeal would be required to refer to the Court of Justice for a preliminary ruling in such cases. The Netherlands declared that it would accept the jurisdiction of the

Court but that it was still considering the further option to be made (see paragraph 8.41).

(ii) Review of the legality of decisions

8.43   Under the existing Treaties, the Court of Justice has extensive powers already to review the legality of Community legislation, but not of acts adopted under the Third Pillar, since these do not form part of Community law. The new Treaty will extend this review jurisdiction of the Court for the first time to acts adopted under the Third Pillar. If a Member State or the Commission, within two months of publication of a framework or other decision takes a case before the Court claiming that such a decision, has been taken illegally the Court will now be able to review its legality.

(iii) Power to rule on disputes

8.44   If a Member State refers a dispute to the Council about the interpretation or the application of an act adopted under the Third Pillar and the Council cannot resolve the dispute within six months, the Court of Justice will now have jurisdiction to rule on the dispute. It will also have jurisdiction to rule on any dispute between Member States and the Commission about the interpretation or the application of conventions.

Authority to conclude international agreements

8.45   Under the existing Treaty there is no provision giving the Union power to conclude international agreements with other States or international organizations on Common Foreign and Security Policy (Second Pillar) or Justice and Home Affairs (Third Pillar) issues. The new Treaty will fill this gap by including a new provision in the CFSP section of the Treaty (see paragraph 15.28).

8.46   This new provision will extend also to the Third Pillar. Where it is necessary to conclude an agreement, the Council, by unanimity, may authorise the Presidency, assisted by the Commission, to open negotiations. At the end of the negotiations, the agreement is to be concluded by the Council, by unanimity, on the recommendation of the Presidency.

8.47   The effect of this is that the agreement, once approved in the Council by unanimity, will not have to be submitted to each Member State for ratification before it comes into force. However, a Member State will not be bound by an agreement if it states in the Council that it must first comply with its own constitutional requirements. At that point other Member States may agree that the agreement applies provisionally to them.

Declaration — no transfer of competence

8.48   A Declaration has been added to meet the position of some Member States who were concerned that these provisions or an agreement reached under them might be read as implying that the Member States were transferring competence for the area in question from national to Union level. The Declaration states that this will not be the case.

Expenditure

8.49   At present the EU Treaty provision in regard to Third Pillar expenditure is as follows:

(i) **administrative expenditure** is charged to the Community budget. (This makes sense because the Third Pillar and the Community as such are served by a single institutional framework)

(ii) for **operational expenditure** which arises in implementing the provisions of the Treaty the Council has an option — it may either:

(a) decide by unanimity to charge it to the Community budget; or

(b) charge it direct to Member States in accordance with a budgetary scale to be decided.

8.50   The new Treaty provides that operational expenditure, like administrative expenditure, is normally to be charged to the Community budget unless the Council by unanimity, decides otherwise. In such a case it is to be charged to the Member States in accordance with the GNP scale unless the Council unanimuously decides otherwise.

Role of the European Parliament

8.51   Under the existing Treaty provisions, the role of the Parliament in relation to the business of the Third Pillar is not a strong one. It is to be regularly informed by the Presidency and the Commission; the Presidency is to consult it on the principal aspects of activities and to ensure that its views are duly taken into consideration. The Parliament may also ask questions of the Council and make recommendations to it; and each year it is to hold a debate on progress made in implementing the Third Pillar provisions.

8.52   The new Treaty will make one change: it provides that the Council must consult the Parliament before it adopts a framework decision or other decision or the text of a convention [(b), (c) and (d) in paragraph 8.29 above]. This is an advance on the requirement in the existing Treaty to consult the Parliament "*on the principal aspects of activities*". It remains still, however, an obligation to consult — though now on each proposal before a decision is taken. The Parliament will not have the right to block a decision.

Role of the Presidency

8.53   The Second Pillar (CFSP) provisions of the new Treaty relating to the role of the Presidency and of the so-called "troika" as revised, will apply also as appropriate to the Third Pillar. This means that the Presidency will be responsible for implementing decisions of the Union and will represent it internationally. The Presidency will be assisted by the Secretary General of the Council and also, if need be, by the next Member State to hold the Presidency. The Commission is to be fully associated in these tasks. The Council may also appoint a special representative for particular policy issues.

"Closer cooperation" ("Flexibility")

8.54   The new Treaty will add to the EU and the EC Treaties a series of new general provisions which will allow a number of Member States amounting at least to a majority to use the institutions of the Union to develop "closer cooperation" between themselves. The general provisions are explained more fully in Chapter 17. However, for ease of reference the particular provisions which will apply under the Third Pillar are described below. These provisions are without prejudice to the Protocol on Schengen (see Chapter 9).

8.55   When a group of Member States constituting at least a majority request authorization to avail of the Union institutions to set up this kind of "closer cooperation" between themselves, the Council will ask the Commission for its opinion and also forward the request to the European Parliament.

8.56   A decision on whether to grant the authorization requested is to be made by the Council by qualified majority but there is provision for what has been called an "emergency brake" which would ultimately allow any Member State to block a decision. This will operate when a Member State for *"important and stated reasons of national policy"* declares that it intends to oppose the decision. In that case no vote will be taken, which means that there will be no decision approved. However, a qualified majority of the Council may demand that the issue go to the European Council (ie Summit level) for final decision by unanimity. This will mean that the Member State opposed can maintain its veto and block a decision.

8.57   Where a Member State which has not joined such a "closer cooperation" arrangement from the outset asks to join in at a later date, the Commission will give an opinion to the Council within three months; and the Council will decide on the request within four months. A favourable decision will be deemed to have been taken unless, by a qualified majority, the Council decides to hold the request in abeyance. It must then give its reasons and set a deadline for re-examining the proposal later.

8.58 The new Treaty extends the jurisdiction of the Court of Justice to the rules governing "closer cooperation" under the Third Pillar.

Role of the Ombudsman

8.59 The Masstricht Treaty added a provision to the EC Treaty (Article 138e) requiring the European Parliament to appoint an Ombudsman to receive, and enquire into, complaints concerning maladministration in Community institutions or bodies (except for the Court of Justice and the Court of First Instance acting in their judicial roles). The new Treaty will extend the Ombudsman's role to Third Pillar matters.

Other provisions of the Third Pillar which will remain unchanged

8.60 While the new Treaty makes substantial changes to the framework and functioning of Third Pillar cooperation as it now operates under the EU Treaty, there are a number of provisions which will remain unchanged. In order to complete the picture of how the re-structured cooperation will operate these are touched on briefly below.

Committee of Senior Officials (the "K4 Committee")

8.61 The EU Treaty set up an advisory committee of senior officials drawn from Justice and Home Affairs Ministries in the Member States. It is responsible to the Ministers in the Council. This will continue in being. To meet the criticism that there were "too many bureaucratic layers", the committee itself, ahead of Treaty reform, has reduced the number of levels by dispensing with one layer of the working groups which reported to it. This was done at the initiative of Ireland during Ireland's EU Presidency in the second half of 1996.

Representation at international organizations and conferences

8.62 In international bodies and conferences Member States are to defend the common positions which the Union adopts under the Third Pillar. Where only some Member States are members of the body, as in the UN Security Council, they are to keep the other Member States fully informed. The permanent members of the Security Council (ie the UK and France) are to ensure the defence of the positions and the interests of the Union. (These provisions apply to both the Second and the Third Pillars).

"Bridge" to First Pillar

8.63   As in the existing Treaty, it will remain possible for the Council to decide that one or more of the areas for common action under the Third Pillar should be transferred to the First Pillar. The effect of this would be to make the area(s) in question matters of Community law rather than intergovernmental cooperation. The voting provisions (qualified majority or unanimity) to apply to that area in future would be decided at the same time.

8.64   Any such decision would, in the first instance, be taken unanimously by the Council, at the initiative of a Member State or of the Commission and after consulting the European Parliament. It would then have to be adopted by the Member States in accordance with their respective constitutional requirements.

Danish Declaration on possible transfer to First Pillar

8.65   Denmark, in a Declaration, states that under its constitution any such decision would require either a 5/6 majority in its Parliament or both a majority in the Parliament and a majority of voters in a referendum.

CHAPTER NINE

Schengen Protocol

9.1   A Protocol which the new Treaty will annex to both the EU and the EC Treaties will bring the Schengen cooperation system, and the commitments and the decisions made in accordance with it, into the framework of the Treaties where it may be further developed in accordance with the relevant Treaty provisions. This Chapter explains the nature and scope of this Protocol.

9.2   Schengen is the term commonly used to describe a separate intergovernmental framework of cooperation which has developed outside the EC/EU Treaty framework. It is so called after the town in Luxembourg where the initial agreement was signed in 1985.

9.3 The Schengen Agreements provide for a comprehensive series of measures in the following areas with a view to achieving the removal of all police and customs formalities for persons crossing internal borders between participating States:

- the harmonisation of visa and asylum policies;
- police and security co-operation, including cross-border observation and cross-border pursuit;
- the harmonisation of provisions on weapons and ammunition;
- judicial co-operation, including judicial assistance in criminal matters, extradition and matters relating to the enforcement of criminal verdicts;
- the development of a common information system in relation to entry, the granting of visas and police co-operation.

9.4   Schengen cooperation developed primarily because the States involved had come to believe that it would not be possible to develop the EU as a whole as an area of free movement of persons with no border controls. The UK was not prepared to accept the principle of lifting controls at its ports of entry from Continental EU Member States. Ireland took a similar position so that it could maintain the Common Travel Area with the UK.

9.5   Thirteen Member States of the EU are now involved in Schengen co-operation to a greater or lesser extent and Norway and Iceland have also signed an agreement to become associated with it. The system is largely in operation and a good deal has been achieved in its development and implementation. The process has, however, not been without its own difficulties and problems have arisen from time to time between the participating States.

9.6   Nevertheless, despite what they have achieved between themselves, the Schengen countries were concerned at this stage to bring their cooperation firmly within the legal and institutional framework of the EU/EC Treaties where they believe it will be more open and accountable and will offer better guarantees for individual rights.

Summary of what the Protocol will do

9.7   What the new Protocol will do may be summarised briefly as follows. What has already been done or agreed in Schengen will now become part of the EC/EU Treaties for the thirteen countries involved. They will also be allowed to build further on it , within the framework of the Treaties, and subject now to their provisions. Ireland and the UK will not be bound by what has already been agreed in Schengen but each of them will be able to opt in to some or all of what has already been done and to take part in any new proposals to build further on it — subject to terms and conditions set out in the Protocol. Special agreements will be negotiated to associate Norway and Iceland with these arrangements.

9.8   The provisions of the Protocol, summarised in the preceding paragraph, are explained in greater detail below.

Details of the Protocol

9.9   The Protocol draws on the concept of "closer cooperation" ("flexibility") which has been introduced elsewhere into the new Treaty and which has been referred to in the account of the restructuring of the Third Pillar given in Chapter 8.

9.10   Its first Article will authorise the thirteen Schengen countries, using the institutional and legal framework of the EU, and respecting the relevant EU and EC Treaty provisions, to establish "closer cooperation" between themselves within the scope of the Schengen agreements and related provisions.

Implementation

9.11   A second Article provides that, from the date of entry into force of the new Treaty, Schengen provisions and the decisions taken to date in Schengen will become part of the EC/EU Treaty framework for those countries and the Council will take on the function of the Schengen Executive Committee. The measures needed to give effect to this. will be taken by the Council acting with the unanimity of the thirteen Schengen countries. In effect therefore, the implementing decisions will be a matter for the Schengen group. However, it is the Council as a whole — ie all fifteen Members — which will decide by unanimity what is to be the appropriate legal basis for each of the Schengen provisions and decisions now being brought into the Treaties. (This cumulative body of commitments and decisions, which is listed in an annex to the Protocol, is described as the "Schengen *acquis*"). In relation to these matters the Court of Justice will exercise the powers conferred on it under the relevant provisions of the Treaties.

Determining the legal basis

9.12   Determining the legal basis means deciding where in the Union structure to fit in the provisions of the Schengen Agreements and the decisions already taken in Schengen. Are they to be part of the EC Treaty and thus part of Community law or are they to be part of the EU Treaty and thus fit into the largely intergovernmental cooperation of the Third Pillar? and, once that is decided, with what provisions exactly in the relevant Treaty will they be associated?

9.13   The Protocol provides a fall-back arrangement. Until the necessary decisions on where to fit them into the Union structure have been taken, the Schengen provisions and the Schengen decisions will be regarded as coming under the Third Pillar. However, in a Declaration in regard to the Protocol the Member States commit themselves not to delay in making the final decisions — they agree that the preparatory work will be undertaken in good time and that the implementing decisions and the decisions on the legal basis will be taken as soon as the new Treaty enters into force.

Position of Denmark on the legal basis

9.14   It seems likely that when the legal basis of the various Schengen decisions comes to be decided, some will be brought into the new Title on freedom of movement, immigration, asylum etc. which will now be part of the EC Treaty (see Chapter 6). Denmark is committed to Schengen cooperation but under a special Protocol it has an opt out which allows it not to participate in the new Title (see Chapter 7). For this reason a special article was incorporated into the Schengen Protocol to protect Denmark's position. It provides that where some of the Schengen decisions are placed in the new Title (in which Denmark will not be a participant), Denmark's rights and obligations in relation to the other twelve countries of the Schengen group will remain unchanged; and when they are placed in the Third Pillar, Denmark will continue to have the same rights and obligations as the other Schengen countries.

Positions of Ireland and of the UK

9.15   It has also been necessary to provide for the positions of Ireland and of the UK since neither country has signed up to the Schengen agreements. Two issues arise: (i) what is to be the position of both countries in relation to what has already been done in Schengen, now that it is being brought into the Treaties? and (ii) what is to be their position in regard to proposals to build further on this within the Treaty structure?

(i) Existing Schengen decisions

9.16   The Protocol provides in Article 4 that the two countries may at any time ask to take part in some or all of what has been done in Schengen to date, which is now to be within the EC/EU Treaty system. Under the provisions which will apply, the Council will decide on the request. Unanimity of the thirteen Schengen States, together with the country making the request (ie Ireland or the UK or both) will be necessary.

9.17   Because of a concern expressed by both Ireland and the UK that a positive decision on such a request might at some future time be blocked by a single contrary vote of one of the thirteen Schengen countries, it was agreed before the new Treaty was signed to make a special Declaration by way of reassurance.

9.18   The Declaration strikes a positive tone about allowing Ireland or the UK to opt in to all or part of the Schengen "acquis". In the Declaration, the parties to the Treaty (ie all of the Member States) invite the Council to seek the opinion of the Commission before deciding on any such request. They also *"undertake to make their best efforts with a view to allowing"* Ircland or the UK, if they so wish, to use the provision for an opt-in so that the Council may be in a position to take the relevant decisions at the date the Treaty enters into force or at any future time.

(ii) Building on the Schengen "acquis"

9.19   Article 5 of the Protocol deals with the question of building on the Schengen *acquis* after it is brought into the Treaty. It provides that proposals and initiatives to this effect shall be subject to the relevant Treaty provisions. This fits with the overall approach of the Protocol. Even though these decisions and commitments were reached originally in a separate framework (Schengen) they will now form part of the EC/EU Treaty framework and it is logical that any proposal to develop them further should be governed by the other relevant provisions of the Treaties.

9.20   While this provision is expressed in general terms, in context it refers particularly to the new "closer cooperation" provisions which will form part of the overall Treaty framework once the new Treaty comes into force. As explained elsewhere in this White Paper those provisions set out the general terms and conditions on which a more limited group of Member States may be authorised to use the institutional framework of the EC/EU for closer cooperation between themselves. The arrangements in the Schengen Protocol can be seen as a specific application of these new provisions.

Advance authorization for "closer cooperation"

9.21 Article 5 of the Protocol has the effect of authorising the thirteen Schengen countries in advance to undertake such "closer cooperation" when necessary to build further on the Schengen *acquis*. It does this by providing that where either Ireland or the UK or both have *not* notified the Presidency "*within a reasonable period*" that they wish to take part in a proposal to build on the Schengen acquis, the thirteen Schengen countries (and Ireland or the UK if either wishes to participate) "*shall be deemed to have been granted*" the necessary authorization under the relevant EC or Third Pillar provision to go ahead without them.

9.22 The Article thus envisages three possible cases which may arise when a proposal is put forward to build further on the Schengen *acquis* within the Treaty framework:

(i) **Ireland and the UK both indicate their wish to take part**. In that case the proposal involves all fifteen Member States and it is dealt with in the Council in the normal way in accordance with the Treaty provision under which it was made (EC or EU /Third Pillar as the case may be);

(ii) **Ireland and the UK do not indicate within a reasonable time that they wish to take part.** In that case the other thirteen (ie the Schengen countries) are deemed under the Protocol to have advance authorization to go ahead without them, using the "closer cooperation" provisions of the new Treaty;

(iii) **Either Ireland or the UK, but not both, indicates its wish to take part.** In that case the authorization for "closer cooperation" is deemed to have been given to the fourteen Member States which wish to go ahead.

9.23 In a Declaration referring to this Article, the signatories of the Treaty undertake "*to make all efforts*" to make action by all fifteen together possible especially whenever Ireland and the UK have accepted some or all of the Schengen *acquis*.

72

Positions of Iceland and Norway

9.24   Article 6 of the Protocol deals with the position of Iceland and Norway. Both countries already signed an agreement in December 1996 associating themselves with Schengen cooperation. The Protocol provides that, on the basis of that agreement, they are to be associated with the implementation and further development of the Schengen *acquis* now that it is being brought within the Treaties. This will be done by a new Agreement (which will include financial provisions) negotiated between those two countries and the Council acting with the unanimity of the thirteen Schengen countries.

9.25   Since Ireland and the UK were not party to the December 1996 agreement but may now take part in some of the Schengen *acquis,* a separate agreement will be needed to establish what rights and obligations will arise in the new situation between Ireland and the UK on the one hand and Iceland and Norway on the other. This will be concluded by the Council, which, in this matter, will act by unanimity of all fifteen Member States.

9.26   In a Declaration referring to this Article, the parties to the Treaty (that is all fifteen Member States) agree *"to take all necessary steps"* so that the two Agreements mentioned may come into force at the same time as the Protocol. This will mean in practice that the negotiation of the new Agreements will need to be done in the period between signature of the new Treaty (2 October 1997) and its entry into force (which will happen when all fifteen Member States have ratified it).

Integration of Schengen Secretariat

9.27   The Schengen Secretariat is to be integrated into the General Secretariat of the Council. Article 7 provides that the Council will decide by qualified majority on the steps needed for this.

Applicants for membership of the Union

9.28   A final Article in the Protocol stipulates that States applying for admission to the Union, when they come to negotiate for membership, must accept the Schengen *acquis* and any further measures which may now be undertaken by the EC/EU institutions within its scope. This reflects a strong wish on the part of a majority of Member States to have agreed provisions on border controls and related issues firmly in place by then and to make it obligatory for all new Members to commit themselves to them.

9.29   In contrast, the thirteen other Member States have, in effect, recognised and accepted in practice the specific and exceptional character of Ireland and the UK as countries with a different approach to controls at ports of entry which is based largely on their island status. These two countries may choose, under the terms of the Protocol, what they will accept of the Schengen *acquis* and how far they will participate in its further development within the Treaties. No such latitude is, however, to be allowed to new Members joining the Union.

CHAPTER TEN

Protocol on asylum for nationals of EU Member States

10.1   During the negotiation of the new Treaty, Spain pressed strongly to have provisions included which would bar nationals of a Member State from seeking asylum in another. It argued that the commitment between Member States which their common membership in the Union implies and the guarantees of rights and freedoms which exist, or will exist under the Treaties, after the entry into force of the Treaty of Amsterdam, make it virtually unthinkable, and indeed offensive, that any Member State should seriously entertain an application for asylum by a national of another Member State.

10.2   Many other Member States, though they understood Spain's concerns, were concerned to meet their obligations under the 1951 Geneva Convention on the Status of Refugees. The Convention, among other things, imposes an obligation to consider each such application individually and on its merits.

10.3   At the conclusion of the negotiations a text was agreed which sets out, in a Protocol to the EC Treaty, the conditions under which an application for asylum by a national of a Member State may be considered by any other Member State. However, it will not affect the legal obligation on Member States under the 1951 Geneva Convention on the Status of Refugees, and the 1967 New York Protocol, to consider each asylum application individually and on its merits.

10.4   The Protocol attached to the new Treaty has a single Article. It provides that, in asylum matters, Member States shall regard each other as *"safe countries of origin"*. Accordingly, an application for asylum by a national of one Member State may be taken into consideration or admitted for processing by another Member State only if one of four conditions is met. These are as follows:

    (a) if the Member State of which the applicant is a national derogates from its obligations under the European Convention on Human Rights;

    (b) if the sanctions procedure provided for in the new Treaty alleging *"a serious and persistent"* breach of the principles of liberty, democracy, respect for human rights and fundamental freedoms and the rule of law (see Chapter 4) has been initiated against the Member State in question;

(c) if a determination has been made that such a serious and persistent breach actually exists;

(d) if a Member State decides unilaterally to entertain the application. In that case the Council is to be informed and the application is to be dealt with on a presumption that it is *"manifestly unfounded"* without, however, affecting in any way the power of the Member State to make a decision on the application.

Declarations

10.5   Three Declarations referring to this Protocol have been made:

(i) A Declaration by all the signatories states that the Protocol does not prejudice the right of each Member State to take the organisational measures it deems necessary to fulfill its obligations under the 1951 Geneva Convention on the Status of Refugees;

(ii) Another Declaration, again by all the signatories, indicates that the question of abuse of asylum procedures in general and the question of appropriate rapid procedures to dispense with manifestly unfounded applications should be further examined. The aim would be to introduce improvements to accelerate these procedures;

(iii) Belgium has made a national Declaration referring to its obligations under the 1951 Convention and the 1967 Protocol . Belgium declares that it will carry out an individual examination of any asylum request made by a national of another Member State.

10.6   The terms of the asylum Protocol itself will allow the Member States to meet their obligations under the 1951 Convention and the 1967 Protocol. The provision in the asylum Protocol that Member States of the Union are to be regarded as *"safe countries of origin"* is compatible with the Convention; and item (d) above, as well as the first Declaration by all Member States, make it clear that they preserve their right — and their obligation under the 1951 Convention — to consider each case individually and on its merits. Accordingly, none of the other Member States, including Ireland, has felt it necessary to make a national Declaration on the lines of that made by Belgium.

CHAPTER ELEVEN

Employment and Social Policy

Employment

Background

11.1   Article 2 of the EC Treaty which sets out the task of the Community already includes the aim of *"a high level of employment and of social protection"*. Member States in deciding on their economic policies have always considered achievement of this aim to be of great importance.

11.2   Over recent years, however, there has been anxiety about unemployment and Member States have been aware of the particular concern felt on this score by the citizens of the Union. This was reflected in the views expressed strongly by many Member States during the course of the negotiation of the new Treaty.

11.3   In those negotiations all Member States accepted that creating and sustaining a high level of employment depends on maintaining competitiveness and flexibility in face of economic and technological change and changing patterns of world trade. They recognised too that much of the responsibility must rest at national or regional level and that much has to be done by business itself and at the level of the individual firm.

11.4   While accepting this, however, a large majority of Member States also took the view that the Community and the Member States should develop a coordinated strategy for employment, closely linked with overall economic policy; and there was strong support for the proposal that provisions to make this possible should be added to the EC Treaty.

What the new Treaty provides

11.5   This will now be done. The new Treaty will insert a new Title dealing with the question of employment into the EC Treaty immediately after Title VI which deals with economic and monetary policy.

Economic policy coordination

11.6 The EC Treaty already provides (Article 103) that Member States shall regard their economic policies as a matter of common concern and shall coordinate them in the Council. The Council, by qualified majority, is required to adopt broad economic policy guidelines for the Member States and the Community on the basis of conclusions of the European Council and it is to monitor economic developments in each of the Member States.

11.7 Member States were concerned not to change in any way these provisions on economic policy which form part of the provisions agreed at Maastricht on Economic and Monetary Union. By placing the new Employment Title immediately after those provisions, however, they wanted to emphasise its importance and the need which they saw for consistency between general economic policy and coordination of policy on employment.

Addition to the activities of the Community

11.8 In order to emphasise the importance which is now to be given to employment policy, the new Treaty will make an addition to Article 3 of the EC Treaty where the activities of the Community are set out. These activities will now include the following which, in effect, refers to the new Title to be inserted into the Treaty:

> *"the promotion of coordination between employment policies of the Member States with a view to enhancing their effectiveness by developing a coordinated strategy for employment."*

A coordinated strategy: the workforce

11.9 The new Title itself will recognise that the coordinated strategy at Community and at national level which it seeks to promote must, if it is to succeed, focus also on improving the skills and the adaptability of the workforce. The first Article of the Title provides that, with a view to achieving the objectives defined in the Treaties:

> *"Member States and the Community shall work towards developing a coordinated strategy for employment and particularly for promoting a skilled, trained and adaptable workforce and labour markets responsive to economic change..."*

Role of Member States

11.10 The immediately following Article requires Member States, through their employment policies, to contribute to achieving these objectives in a way consistent with the broad guidelines for the economic policies of Member States and of the Community adopted under the Treaty; they are to regard promoting employment as a matter of common concern; and they are to coordinate their action in regard to it within the Council.

Role of the Community

11.11   A third Article provides that, for its part, the Community as such is to contribute to a high level of employment by encouraging this cooperation between its Member States and by supporting and, if necessary, complementing what they do while respecting the competences of the Member States. The objective of a high level of employment is to be taken into consideration in other Community policies and activities.

11.12   The other Articles in the new Title set out how these aims are to be addressed at each level and the procedure which is to be followed by the Member States and the Community respectively in developing a coordinated employment strategy.

Procedure for strategic coordination

The European Council

11.13   The procedure can be seen as beginning at the highest level with the European Council. Each year, the European Council is to consider the employment situation in the Community and to adopt conclusions. It will do so on the basis of an annual report to be submitted to it jointly by the Council and the Commission.

The Council

11.14   The Council for its part, basing itself on these conclusions, is to draw up guidelines which the Member States will be required to take into account in their national employment policies. The guidelines must be consistent with the broad economic policy guidelines which the Council is also required to adopt in a separate process already provided for in Article 103(2) of the EC Treaty.

11.15   In drawing up these employment policy guidelines, the Council will act by qualified majority, on a Commission proposal and after consulting the European Parliament, the Economic and Social Committee, the Committee of the Regions and the new Employment Committee which is now to be established (see below).

Reports by Member States

11.16   Each Member State will be required to report annually to the Council on the principal measures it has taken during the year to implement employment policy in the light of the guidelines set by the Council.

Consideration by the Council

11.17   In the light of the guidelines, and on the basis of the reports, the Council will each year look at how the Member States have implemented employment policy and, acting by a qualified majority on a Commission recommendation, may make recommendations to Member States in regard to their policies. Drawing all of this together, the Council and the Commission will then make a joint report each year to the European Council on the employment situation in the Community and on the implementation of the employment guidelines.

Incentive measures

11.18   The Council, acting in co-decision with the European Parliament and after consulting the Economic and Social Committee and the Committee of the Regions, may adopt incentive measures.

11.19   Such measures would be designed to encourage cooperation between Member States and to encourage their action on employment. They could include for example exchange of information and best practices; analysis and advice, promoting innovative approaches, pilot projects and so on but they must not include harmonization of the laws/regulations of Member States.

11.20   The idea of providing in the new Treaty for such incentive measures, while important to most Member States, caused concern to one or two others who feared that it could lead to large expenditure. These concerns were met by adding a Declaration in which all Member States agreed that any incentive measures taken should always specify the grounds, the duration and the maximum cost of the measures being undertaken.

Employment Committee

11.21   Finally the new Title provides that the Council is to establish an advisory Employment Committee to promote coordination between Member States on employment and labour market policies. It is also to monitor the employment situation and employment policies in the Member States and across the Community and to offer advice and formulate opinions. In doing so it is required to consult the social partners, that is management and labour.

11.22   While the new Treaty was being negotiated, the Council itself decided to establish an Employment Committee. The inclusion of a specific provision in the new Treaty about an Employment Committee, the context in which it is placed and the role explicitly assigned to it, will, however, provide a stronger base for such a Committee to play an important role on the employment issue.

11.23   The Committee for which the new Treaty provides will have two members from each Member State and from the Commission. Although this is not spelled out in the text, the underlying idea is that Member States will be free to appoint an expert on economic policy issues as one member and a specialist in labour issues as the other. If constituted in this way, the Employment Committee could become a forum where both kinds of policies could interact. In this way tensions could be sorted out and greater consistency of approach established before the issues come to Council level.

Social Policy

11.24   The term "Social Policy" is used to cover a number of issues including in particular labour law and working conditions, aspects of employment and vocational training and social security.

Background — the present position

11.25   Title VIII in the EC Treaty deals with *"Social Policy, Education, Vocational Training and Youth"*. Chapter 1 of this Title, which is headed *"Social Provisions"*, is usually called the "Social Chapter". It touches on such matters as the promotion of improved working conditions, social protection, equal pay for equal work and the desirability of dialogue at European level between management and labour. Chapter 2 deals with the European Social Fund and Chapter 3 (added by the Maastricht Treaty) contains provisions on *"Education, Vocational Training and Youth"*.

The Social Protocol and the Social Agreement — the UK opt out

11.26   In the course of the negotiations which led up to the Maastricht Treaty of 1992, most Member States wished to add various provisions to develop the Social Chapter. However, the UK would not accept these changes. A compromise was reached by the Heads of State or Government at Maastricht itself. This involved keeping the proposed amendments out of the new Treaty and incorporating them instead in a separate agreement subscribed to by all the eleven other Member States. (The membership at the time was twelve). This Social Agreement was accepted also by Austria, Finland and Sweden when they joined the EU in 1994.

11.27   The result has been to create a rather complex arrangement so far as the additional social provisions are concerned. A Social Protocol, accepted by all Member States, including the UK, has been part of the EC Treaty since

Maastricht. It authorises all of the other Member States (originally eleven, now fourteen) to use the Treaty institutions to apply between themselves this separate Social <u>Agreement</u> which contains the social provisions which the UK refused to accept. The effect in practice can be said to be to allow an "opt-out" from such provisions to the UK.

11.28   Most Member States regarded this as a very unsatisfactory situation but felt that there had been no option but to accept it at Maastricht. They hoped, however, to see it changed in the new Treaty. At first the UK was unwilling, but following the election on 1 May 1997, the new British Government decided to end the UK opt out and to accept that the provisions of the Social Agreement should now apply to all fifteen Member States.

What the new Treaty will do

11.29   This is given effect in the new Treaty. Under its terms the provisions of the Social Agreement, now adapted further in various ways, are brought into the main body of the EC Treaty where they replace a number of the Articles of the existing "Social Chapter" (see paragraph 11.25 above). These provisions, which until now committed fourteen Member States only, including Ireland, will become Community law for all fifteen Member States. The effect is to end the breach on Social Policy between the UK and the other fourteen Member States which opened up at Maastricht and which has lasted for five years.

11.30   In bringing the Social Agreement into the main body of the EC Treaty and extending its application to all fifteen Member States, the new Treaty will also adapt the provisions of the Agreement in certain ways. The terms of the Social Agreement, as it stands, already apply to Ireland. For the sake of clarity, however, the account given below will summarise not just the new elements but how the Social Chapter in the EC Treaty will read after the Social Agreement has been incorporated and after the other amendments have been made.

Statement of objectives

11.31   As amended, the Social Chapter in the EC Treaty will now open with a general statement of objectives. Its first Article (Article 117 of the EC Treaty), drawn largely from Article 1 of the Social Agreement, will begin with a reference to fundamental social rights such as those in the European Social Charter of 1961 and the Community Charter of the Fundamental Social Rights of Workers of 1989. It then sets as objectives for the Community and the Member States:

> *"the promotion of employment, improved living and working conditions, so as to make possible their harmonization while the improvement is being maintained,*

proper social protection, dialogue between management and labour, the develop-
ment of human resources with a view to lasting high employment and the combating
of exclusion."

11.32   To achieve these objectives, the Community and the Member States are
to implement measures which take account of the diverse forms of national
practice, in particular in the field of contractual relations, and the need to
maintain the competitiveness of the Community economy.

How the objective is to be achieved

11.33   The Articles which follow will set out in greater detail how the objective
set is to be achieved, dealing successively with what is to be done by the Community through the Council, by the Commission and by the Member States.

11.34   As already provided in the Social Agreement, the Community, under
the new Article 118, is to support and complement the activities of the Member
States in a number of listed areas. These include improvement of working conditions and of the working environment in the interest of workers' health and
safety, information and consultation of workers, integration of persons
excluded from the labour market and equality of opportunity, and at work,
between men and women. However, the Article is not to apply to pay, the right
of association and the right to strike or to lock out. A separate Article — Article
119 — deals with the principle of equal pay for men and women (see paragraphs
11.46-11.48 below).

Decision-making procedure

11.35   The Council, acting in co-decision with the European Parliament and
after consulting the Economic and Social Committee, may, in the areas referred
to, adopt directives and set minimum requirements to be implemented gradu-
ally (under the Social Agreement, the procedure in relation to the European
Parliament was cooperation rather than co-decision). In doing so, it should,
however, take account of the conditions in each Member State and should avoid
imposing constraints in a way which would hamper small and medium sized
enterprises or discriminate unjustifiably against them.

11.36   The Council action envisaged here is to be seen as setting minimum
standards. It remains open to Member States to maintain or introduce more
stringent protective measures at the national level provided they are compatible
with the Treaty.

11.37   Co-decision, as provided for in this case, involves qualified majority voting in the Council. The Council is, however, to act unanimously, after consulting the Parliament, in a certain number of areas. These include social security and social protection of workers (other than programmes for social exclusion

— see paragraph 11.40 below); protection of workers whose employment contract is terminated; representation and collective defence of the interests of workers and employers; employment conditions for foreign nationals resident in the Community; and financial contributions to promote job-creation.

Possible role for management and labour

11.38   In adopting a directive the Council in effect prescribes, in a binding way, the result to be achieved in Member States but it leaves it to the individual Member States to decide how exactly they are to achieve it. In the case of the Council directives referred to here, a Member State may entrust implementation to management and labour if they jointly request this but the Member State retains ultimate responsibility for seeing that it is carried through.

Social exclusion

11.39   This Article as amended by the new Treaty will now also contain a provision on social exclusion. This was a matter of particular interest to Ireland during the negotiation of the new Treaty and the text results from a proposal which Ireland put forward. Social exclusion refers to the situation of persons who are not merely unemployed but marginalised and living in poverty through deprivation of various kinds, including family breakdown, substance abuse and homelessness and who, because of their situation, are excluded from the workforce and from social and community networks.

11.40   Three EC pilot programmes to address the causes of poverty and social exclusion, in which Ireland participated, were completed successfully. However, it did not prove possible to get unanimous agreement on a fourth programme. Doubts were also raised about how far there was a clear legal basis for such action in the Treaty. With the amendments made by the new Treaty, the EC Treaty will now, for the first time, contain an explicit legal basis for action on social exclusion. This will permit the Council to adopt measures to encourage cooperation between Member States to combat social exclusion through initiatives aimed at improving knowledge, evaluating experiences and promoting innovative approaches and exchanges of information and best practices. In putting its proposal forward, Ireland argued that such incentive measures could be very beneficial but need not necessarily involve large additional financial costs. Unanimity in the Council will no longer be necessary for the adoption of such measures. Voting, in future, will be by qualified majority in the Council and the measures will be adopted in conjunction with the European Parliament under the co-decision procedure.

Dialogue between the social partners

11.41   Article 118b of the EC Treaty as it stands already provides that the Commission is to try to develop the dialogue between management and labour at European level *"which could, if the two sides consider it desirable, lead to relations based on agreement."* The much more developed provisions of the Social Agreement on this point which are now to be brought fully into the Treaty will augment and develop further this positive reference to dialogue.

11.42   Under these provisions (which will become Article 118a of the EC Treaty), the Commission has the task of promoting consultation of management and labour at Community level and facilitating their dialogue in a balanced way. It is to consult them on the possible direction of Community action, and again on the content, before it submits a proposal to the Council.

11.43   The existing Treaty provides (in Article 118b) that if management and labour so desire, the dialogue between them at Community level may lead to contractual relations, including agreements. The Treaty proper will now incorporate the more extensive provisions of the Social Agreement in a revised Article 118b. As to implementation of these agreements at Community level, these provisions will offer a choice: it may be left to the normal practices of management and labour and the Member States; or, if the parties signing the agreement — that is management and labour — jointly request this, it may be made the subject of a Council decision, adopted by qualified majority or by unanimity, according to the subject matter.

11.44   According to a Declaration referring to these provisions, the first application of this latter provision will consist in developing the content of the relevant agreements by collective bargaining according to the rules of each Member State.

Cooperation between Member States

11.45   With a view to achieving the objectives set for the Social Policy (see paragraph 11.31 above) the Commission is also to encourage cooperation between the Member States and to facilitate the coordination of their action in all the social policy fields referred to — through studies, opinions and consultations. This will apply particularly to matters relating to employment, labour law and working conditions, vocational training, social security, prevention of occupational accidents and diseases, occupational hygiene and the rights of association and collective bargaining between employers and workers. These provisions combine the formulation in the Social Agreement with what is already in the main body of the EC Treaty.

Equal pay for equal work or work of equal value

11.46   Under the EC Treaty as it stands, (Article 119) Member States are already required to apply the principle of equal pay for equal work as between men and women. The new provisions now to be inserted develop this principle further by adding the phrase *"or work of equal value"*. This wording reflects the interpretation by the Court of Justice of the existing text of Article 119. Drawing on the Social Agreement, the new provisions also define such terms as *"equal pay without discrimination based on sex"* and they spell out in detail how the principle is to be applied.

11.47   Each Member State is to *"ensure that the principle of equal pay for equal work or work of equal value"* (as defined), is applied. A Member State will be allowed to maintain or adopt measures of positive action to redress imbalances between the sexes. The wording here is impartial as between men and women. A Declaration attached indicates, however, that the aim in the first instance should be to improve the situation of women in working life.

11.48   The new Treaty, by adding these provisions to the EC Treaty, will take an important step in this area, which will go beyond what is provided at present either in the EC Treaty or the Social Agreement. It will provide a new legal basis for action by the Council. The EC Treaty as amended will now require the Council to adopt measures *"to ensure the application of the principle of equal opportunities and equal treatment of men and women in matters of employment and occupation, including the principle of equal pay for equal work or work of equal value"*. In adopting such measures the Council is to consult the Economic and Social Committee and it is to act in co-decision with the European Parliament, a procedure which will involve qualified majority voting in the Council.

Annual report by the Commission

11.49   At present, the EC Treaty provides that the Commission is to include a chapter on social developments within the Community in its annual report to the European Parliament. The new Treaty will strengthen this considerably by incorporating the much fuller provisions of the Social Agreement. The EC Treaty, thus amended, will now require the Commission to draw up a report each year on progress in achieving the objectives set out for Social Policy (see paragraph 11.31 above), including the demographic situation in the Community. The Commission is to forward this report to the European Parliament, the Council and the Economic and Social Committee. The Parliament may also invite the Commission to report on particular problems.

CHAPTER TWELVE

Environment, Public Health and Consumer Policies

Environment

Background — the present position

12.1   There is already a separate Title on the Environment in the EC Treaty. It provides that Community policy on the environment is to pursue four objectives: preserving and improving the quality of the environment; protecting public health; prudent and rational use of resources; and promotion of measures at international level to deal with problems.

12.2   Community policy is required to aim at a high level of protection of the environment while taking into account the diversity of various regions. It is to be based on the precautionary principle, on the principles of preventive action and remedy at source as a priority and on the principle that the polluter should pay. The Treaty also stipulates that environmental protection requirements must be integrated into the definition and implementation of other Community policies.

12.3   Protection of the environment is also one of a limited number of grounds on which, subject to certain limitations, and subject in particular to confirmation by the Commission, a Member State may be allowed to apply stricter national measures after the Council, by a qualified majority, has adopted harmonisation measures under the internal market provisions of the EC Treaty (Art. 100a.4).

12.4   The national measures in question must be reported to the Commission and they are subject to confirmation by it. The Commission is required to confirm that they are not a means of arbitrary discrimination or a disguised restriction on trade between Member States. They may also be challenged before the Court of Justice by a Member State or by the Commission.

12.5   The fact that, subject to these conditions, a Member State may be allowed to continue applying stricter national provisions on environmental grounds even after adoption of an internal market harmonisation measure, has been controversial — both for those who wanted greater latitude to introduce national measures if necessary to protect the environment and for those who feared that such provisions might damage the internal market.

What the new Treaty will do

Summary

12.6   The new Treaty will amend these EC Treaty provisions and some of the provisions of the EU Treaty so as to give greater emphasis to sustainable development and to the aim of protecting the environment . It will also amend substantially the existing EC Treaty provision under which a Member State in certain circumstances may be allowed to apply stricter national measures after the Council has adopted an internal market harmonisation measure. These changes are described in more detail in the following paragraphs.

Amendment of EU Treaty — sustainable development

12.7   There will be two changes to the EU Treaty which will emphasise *"sustainable development"*:

(i)   a reference to *"the principle of sustainable development"* will be added to the paragraph of the Preamble in which Member States express their determination to promote certain aims in the Union;

(ii)   a reference to achieving *"balanced and sustainable development"*, (a term endorsed at the Rio Earth Summit) will be added to Article B of the EU Treaty in which the Union sets its objectives.

Amendment of EC Treaty

12.8   The EC Treaty is also to be amended in ways which will give rather greater emphasis to environmental concerns.

12.9   At present Article 2 in referring to the task of the Community, speaks of the promotion throughout the Community of *"...a harmonious and balanced development of economic activities, sustainable and non-inflationary growth respecting the environment..."*. The text as amended will now refer to the promotion throughout the Community of *"a harmonious, balanced and sustainable development of economic activities"* and, at a later point, it will refer to *"a high level of protection and improvement of the quality of the environment"*. The reference to sustainable and non-inflationary growth will also be retained.

12.10   As in the case of the changes to the EU Treaty mentioned above, this change is intended to emphasise sustainable development and environmental concerns by using stronger and more generally accepted formulations.

The integration principle

12.11   A second change to the EC Treaty relates to the placing in the Treaty of the so-called "integration principle" which is expressed in the Treaty as a requirement that *"environmental protection requirements must be integrated into the definition and implementation of other Community policies."*

12.12   In the EC Treaty, as it stands, this sentence is included as one of a number of points in Article 130r in Title XVI which deals with the Environment. The new Treaty will amend the EC Treaty so as to bring this principle "up front". It will be strengthened slightly and transferred to the opening provisions of the Treaty as Article 3c in order that it will have greater prominence and be seen to govern all of the provisions of the Treaty.

Commission environmental impact assessments

12.13   Furthermore the Commission is now to prepare environmental impact assessment studies whenever it makes proposals which may have significant environmental implications. A Declaration notes that the Commission has undertaken to do this.

Authorization to apply national provisions

12.14   A substantial change will be made to those provisions of the EC Treaty relating to the internal market which allow a Member State, subject to confirmation by the Commission, to apply existing national measures on environmental and other specified grounds after an internal market harmonisation measure has been adopted. These were of concern since some Member States consider that their national standards in environmental matters are higher than those which have been, or are likely to be, agreed at Community level.

12.15   First, a change will be made in the language which provides that the Commission in its internal market proposals concerning health, safety, environmental protection and consumer protection, *"will take as a base a high level of protection"*. This is now to be amended to add the phrase *"taking account in particular of any new development based on scientific facts."* This provision referring to the Commission is also fleshed out further by adding a new sentence: *"Within their respective powers, the European Parliament and the Council will also seek to achieve this objective."*

12.16   A second change will extend the circumstances in which a Member State may be allowed to apply national provisions (Art. 100a.4). The present Treaty envisages that this might arise "*after the adoption of a harmonisation measure by the Council acting by a qualified majority*" (emphasis added). During the negotiations, Denmark and Sweden in particular expressed strongly a concern that this wording was too limiting.

12.17   To meet this concern it was agreed that the new Treaty will change the wording here in two respects: (a) the reference to a qualified majority will be dropped; and (b) a reference to the Commission will be added to cover a case where the Commission may adopt a harmonisation measure. The text as amended will now read "*If, after the adoption by the Council or the Commission of a harmonisation measure...*"

12.18   The main changes in this Article are substantive changes in regard to the possible application of stricter national measures by a Member State after an internal market measure has been adopted. The EC Treaty at present speaks of a situation where, after a harmonisation measure, "*a Member State deems it necessary to apply national provisions*" on grounds which include protection of the environment. While the word "*apply*" may seem ambiguous here, it has not generally been read as permitting the introduction of new national provisions, as distinct from the maintenance of those which already exist.

Introducing or applying national provisions

12.19   The new Treaty will amend this provision of the EC Treaty so that it will now address two possible cases:

(i) the case where, after adoption of a harmonisation measure by the Council or the Commission, a Member State "*deems it necessary to maintain national provisions*";

and

(ii) the case where, after adoption of a harmonisation measure by the Council or the Commission, a Member State "*deems it necessary to introduce national provisions based on new scientific evidence relating to the protection of the environment or the working environment on grounds of a problem specific to that Member State, arising after the adoption of the harmonisation measure*".

(emphasis added in both cases)

12.20   The explicit acceptance in the second case of the idea that a Member State might introduce new national provisions, as distinct from maintaining some or all of those which it already had in place before the Community harmonisation measures were brought in, is new but it is subject to qualifications.

The provisions must be based on new scientific evidence; the problem must be specific to that Member State; and it must have arisen after the adoption of the harmonisation measure.

Commission is to decide

12.21 In either of the two cases the Commission is to be notified of the national measures and told why they are needed. Within six months of this notification, the Commission is to approve or reject them. Before doing so it must check that they are not a means of arbitrary discrimination, a disguised restriction on trade between Member States or (and this is a new qualification) an obstacle to the functioning of the internal market. If the Commission has not given a decision within six months the national provisions will be deemed to have been approved but if the matter is complex and there is no danger to human health, the Commission may extend the period within which it has to make its decision for an additional six months.

12.22 Furthermore, if it does authorise a Member State to introduce or maintain national provisions in this way, then the Commission must immediately examine whether to propose an adaptation to the measure as it applies to the Community as a whole. The logic of this is that the *"new scientific evidence"* which has become available to the Member State might also show the need for corresponding change at Community level.

12.23 Where the Member State raises a problem on public health grounds, the Commission is also to examine whether to propose measures to the Council.

Action in Court of Justice

12.24 As is the case under the existing Treaty, it will be possible for any Member State or the Commission to bring a case direct to the Court of Justice if it considers that another Member State is making improper use of the powers available to it under the Article.

Public Health

Background — the present position

12.25 The EC Treaty already contains a separate Title (Title X) dealing with Public Health. It envisages the role of the Community in this area as primarily to encourage and support what is done by Member States.

12.26   This is made clear in the single Article (129) of the Title. It provides that the Community shall contribute towards a high level of human health protection by encouraging cooperation between Member States and, if necessary supporting their action. Community action is to be directed towards disease prevention, particularly the major health scourges including drug dependence, by promoting research and health information and education. Health protection requirements are to be part of the Community's other policies. Member States, in liaison with the Commission, are to coordinate their policies among themselves and wider international cooperation is to be fostered.

12.27   To contribute to the objectives of the Title the Council is to adopt incentive measures and recommendations. Incentive measures are to be adopted by the Council in co-decision with the European Parliament after consulting the Economic and Social Committee and the Committee of the Regions but the Council may not prescribe any harmonisation of the laws and regulations of the Member States. Recommendations are to be adopted by the Council by qualified majority, on a proposal from the Commission.

Reasons for change

12.28   During the negotiation of the new Treaty it was evident that Member States were very concerned about the dangers to human health throughout the Community from diseases such as BSE; about safety standards in relation to the medical use of human organs and blood; and about the health damage resulting from drug dependency. For these reasons, there was a general wish to develop and add to the provisions relating to cooperation on public health matters already contained in the EC Treaty while at the same time fully respecting the responsibilities of Member States in such highly sensitive areas as health services and medical care.

What the new Treaty will do

Summary

12.29   The new Treaty will amend and develop the existing provisions on public health in the EC Treaty (Article 129). The basic thrust of the present provisions will remain but the amendments will allow the Community to set safety standards in relation to human organs and blood and to take measures specifically to protect human health against animal and plant diseases. The Treaty will, however, continue to recognise that fundamental responsibility in health and medical care matters must remain at Member State level.

Role of Community action

12.30   The Article as amended will begin by stating that a high level of human health protection is to be ensured in the definition and implementation of all Community policies and activities. Member States, in liaison with the Commission, are to coordinate their policies and programmes (as already provided in the existing Treaty). The role of the Community will be to complement what is done at national level and, with the Member States, to foster wider international cooperation.

12.31   Community action will be directed towards improving public health and preventing disease — particularly the major health scourges — through promoting research and health information and education. It will also complement what is done by Member States to reduce and prevent drug-related health damage, including information and prevention.

Adoption of measures by the Council

12.32   The Council, acting in co-decision with the European Parliament (which will involve qualified majority voting in the Council) and after consulting the Economic and Social Committee and the Committee of the Regions, is to contribute to the objectives set out in the Article by adopting measures in three areas:

(a) measures setting high quality and safety standards for human organs and blood and blood derivatives. While these common standards will apply throughout the Community, a Member State which so wishes will be free to maintain or introduce its own higher standards. Furthermore, the measures are not to affect national provisions on the donation or medical use of organs and blood;

(b) measures in relation to plant or animal diseases which have as their direct objective the protection of public health. (An example would be public health measures in relation to BSE.) Purely veterinary or agricultural aspects will, however, continue to be dealt with under the provisions on Agriculture in Title II (Article 43) of the EC Treaty;

(c) incentive measures to protect and improve public health. However, these must not include any harmonization of the laws or regulations of Member States.

12.33   As under the present Treaty, the Council, acting by qualified majority on a Commission proposal, may also adopt recommendations for the purposes of the Article (These will not have binding force).

Respect for the responsibilities of Member States

12.34   The Article explicitly stipulates that Community action in the field of public health shall fully respect the responsibilities of the Member States for the organization and delivery of health services and medical care.

Consumer protection

Background — the present position

12.35   Originally, the EC Treaty did not contain any provisions on consumer protection policies. However, the Single European Act of 1986 in setting out the provisions for the establishment of the Single Market, spoke of the need for a high level of consumer protection. This was developed further when the Maastricht Treaty of 1992 added to the EC Treaty a new Title XI containing a single Article (129a) on Consumer Protection.

12.36   In consequence, the present Treaty provides a legal basis for action by the Community to support and supplement the policy of the Member States in matters relating to the interests of consumers. The Community is to contribute to the attainment of a high level of consumer protection through:

(a) the general measures which it adopts under the Treaty (Article 100a) to complete the internal market; and

(b) specific action on consumer issues in support of the policy of Member States.

12.37   The specific action under (b) is to be adopted in co-decision with the European Parliament after consulting the Economic and Social Committee. The purpose is to protect the health, safety and economic interests of consumers and to provide them with adequate information. Member States remain free, if they so wish, to maintain or introduce more stringent measures of their own provided they are not incompatible with the Treaty. They must notify the Commission if they do so.

Reasons for change

12.38   During the negotiations which led to the new Treaty, Member States agreed on the need to strengthen these provisions somewhat in the interest of consumers, while recognising that much of the responsibility must still remain at national level.

What the new Treaty will do

12.39   The present Article in the EC Treaty which provides for action by the Community in support of national policies will be strengthened by introducing the idea of rights and the idea of consumer education and organization.

12.40   Community action will now be directed not only to protecting the *"health, safety and economic interests of consumers"* and to providing *"adequate information"* (as in the existing text) but also to *"promoting their right to information, education and to organise themselves in order to safeguard their interests"*. (A proposal made during the negotiations to add a reference to protecting the legal rights of consumers was not adopted because it was felt that this was a matter which is better left to the national courts in Member States.)

Consumer protection and other Community policies

12.41   The amended Article will now also include for the first time what is called a "horizontal provision" extending the concept of consumer protection across all areas of Community action. It provides explicitly that *"consumer protection requirements shall be taken into account in defining and implementing other Community policies and activities"*.

12.42   Apart from these two steps to strengthen the Treaty provisions for consumer protection, the other provisions of the existing Article (described above) will remain substantially unchanged.

CHAPTER THIRTEEN

Subsidiarity and Proportionality; Transparency; and Quality of Legislation

Subsidiarity and Proportionality

Background —The present position

13.1   Subsidiarity is a general principle which can be applied in any political system. Essentially it means that decisions should always be taken at the lowest level at which they can be taken effectively and only if the nature of the decision requires it should a decision be referred upwards. In the Community it is seen as a dynamic concept which would allow Community action within the limits of its powers to be expanded where circumstances require this or conversely, restricted or discontinued where it is no longer justified.

13.2   The subsidiarity principle is set out and defined in Article 3b of the EC Treaty which was inserted by the Maastricht Treaty of 1992. The negotiations which led up to agreement on the text of the new article were difficult. Some Member States emphasised what they saw as the need to limit the further extension of the role and powers of the Community. Others accepted the principle of subsidiarity but were concerned to see it very carefully defined lest it be used to block or roll back legitimate action by the Community.

13.3   The Article as eventually agreed and inserted into the Treaty affirms the principle that the Community shall act within the limits of the powers conferred by the Treaty; and that Community action shall not go beyond what is necessary to achieve the objectives of the Treaty.

13.4   The obligation to respect the subsidiarity principle is set out specifically in the Article in the following terms:

"In areas which do not fall within its exclusive competence, the Community shall take action, in accordance with the principle of subsidiarity, only if and in so far as the objectives of the proposed action cannot be sufficiently achieved by the Member States and can therefore, by reason of the scale or effects of the proposed action, be better achieved by the Community."

96

13.5   Two particularly important elements in this formulation may be noted:

    (i) the principle does not apply in areas of action which fall within the exclusive competence of the Community under the Treaty; it applies only to areas of mixed or shared competence where it helps to delimit the respective roles of the Community and of the Member States;

    (ii) A two-sided criterion is to be applied in deciding where Community action is justified: it must be the case (a) that the objectives cannot be sufficiently achieved by the Member States; and (b) that they can therefore be better achieved by the Community because of the scale or effects of the proposed action.

Birmingham and Edinburgh Conclusions

13.6   Since this Article was added to the EC Treaty in 1992 the European Council has agreed conclusions setting out further details on how the principle is to be applied. These appear as conclusions of the Birmingham and Edinburgh meetings of the European Council in 1992.

Reasons for change

13.7   In the course of the negotiations leading to the new Treaty, some Member States — notably Germany, the UK and Austria — wished to see greater prominence given to the application of the subsidiarity principle although they accepted that this should not involve amendment of Article 3b of the EC Treaty. Others were concerned not to re-open unnecessarily the difficult debate on the principle which had preceded agreement in 1992 to insert the new Article 3b.

13.8   These differing emphases were reconciled and accommodated in an agreement to add to the new Treaty a Protocol on the application of the principle of subsidiarity. It was accepted that, as to content, this Protocol would essentially incorporate the conclusions on application of the principle already agreed by all Member States at the Birmingham and Edinburgh European Councils in 1992. They would now, however, have more formal status as a Protocol, which has the same legal status as the Treaty itself.

What the new Treaty will do

13.9   The new Treaty will add a Protocol on the application of the principle of subsidiarity to the EC Treaty. The Protocol confirms the conclusions agreed at Birmingham and Edinburgh and the text is largely based on those conclusions, with some adaptations which proved necessary in turning a political agreement into legal form as a Protocol. The text of the conclusions was also adapted further in certain ways. The focus is still, however, on application of the subsidiarity principle. The principle itself, as formulated in Article 3b of the EC Treaty is explained further but it has not been re-opened or amended.

13.10   The main provisions of the Protocol may be summarised as follows:

(i)   Each of the Community institutions must ensure compliance with the principles of subsidiarity and proportionality (proportionality means that any action by the Community shall not go beyond what is necessary to achieve the objectives of the Treaty);

(ii)   The Treaty provisions and objectives, the *acquis* (that is the cumulative total of commitments and decisions taken over the years) and the institutional balance must be respected in applying the principle of subsidiarity. The principles which the Court of Justice has developed in regard to the relationship between national and Community law are not to be affected;

(iii)   Subsidiarity provides a guide as to how powers at Community level are to be exercised where the Community does not have exclusive competence. It does not call in question the Community's powers under the Treaty as interpreted by the Court;

(iv)   Subsidiarity is a dynamic concept. It allows action by the Community within the limits of its powers to be expanded where necessary or restricted or discontinued where it is no longer justified;

(v)   Any proposal for Community legislation must state the reasons on which it is based so as to show that it complies with subsidiarity and proportionality;

(vi)   There are two aspects to the subsidiarity principle and action by the Community is justified only where both are met. It must be the case that the objectives cannot be sufficiently achieved at national level; and that they can be better achieved at Community level;

(vii)   Guidelines in assessing this are that: transnational aspects to the issue cannot be dealt with at national level; lack of Community action would conflict with Treaty requirements or damage Member States' interests; Community action would produce clear benefits by reason of its scale or effects;

(viii)   The form of Community action should be as simple as possible and it should leave as much scope as possible for national decision. Directives (which are binding as to the result to be attained but leave it to Member States to decide how it is to be achieved) are to be preferred to Regulations (which bind both as to form and result) and framework Directives to detailed measures;

(ix) While respecting Community law, care should also be taken to respect well-established national arrangements and national legal systems;

(x) Where subsidiarity leads to no action by the Community, Member States are still bound by the general obligations of the Treaty and bound to abstain from any measure which could jeopardise its objectives;

(xi) The Commission should as a rule consult widely before proposing legislation; justify the proposal as regards subsidiarity; try to minimise the burdens being imposed; and report annually to the European Council, the Council and the Parliament on the application of the Treaty Article on Subsidiarity (3b).

Declaration on the application of Community law by Member States

13.11   A Declaration by the Member States in regard to the new Protocol confirms a previous Declaration of 1992 which stressed that the measures to be taken by Member States should result in Community law being applied with the same effectiveness and rigour as national law; at the same time the Declaration confirms the conclusions of the Essen European Council in 1994 that the administrative implementation of Community law is in principle the responsibility of Member States in accordance with their constitutional arrangements.

Declaration by Austria, Belgium and Denmark

13.12   A further Declaration was made jointly by Germany, Austria and Belgium. These are all countries which have a highly developed federal structure internally. Their Declaration states their assumption that EC action in accordance with the subsidiarity principle concerns not only Member States as such but also their sub-divisions, to the extent that they have law-making powers.

Transparency

Background — reasons for change

13.13   In recent years, particularly since the Maastricht Treaty of 1992, there has been considerable discussion about the need to make the institutions of the Union more transparent and open and to bring what they do closer to the lives of the individual citizens of the Member States. The need for this was stressed by a number of Member States during the negotiation of the new Treaty — particularly by the Scandinavian countries which at national level have a long tradition of openness and relatively easy access to many kinds of Government documents.

What the New Treaty will do

Decisions close to the citizen

13.14   The new Treaty will amend the opening article of the EU Treaty so as to emphasise the need for greater transparency. The Article at present speaks of the process of creating an ever closer Union *"...in which decisions are taken as closely as possible to the citizen"*. The text will now read *"...in which decisions are taken as openly as possible and as closely as possible to the citizen"*.

Access to EC documents

13.15   The main amendment of substance made by the new Treaty will be to add a new article (Article 191a) to the EC Treaty to provide for greater access to documents of the main institutions. The new Article provides that any citizen of the Union or any person or legal entity residing in it shall have a right of access to European Parliament, Council and Commission documents subject to principles and conditions to be defined.

13.16   The general principles and limits on access are to be laid down by the Council, acting in co-decision with the European Parliament within two years of the entry into force of the new Treaty. Each institution is to elaborate specific provisions in its own rules of procedure regarding access to its own documents.

13.17   The new Treaty will also provide (by amending Article 151 of the EC Treaty) that the Council in its rules of procedure is to define the cases where it is acting in its legislative capacity with a view to allowing greater access to documents in such cases while preserving the effectiveness of its decision-making. In any event, when it acts in a legislative capacity, the results of votes and explanations of vote and statements in the minutes are to be made public.

13.18   In a Declaration the Member States also expressed the view that the European Parliament, the Council and the Commission, when acting in European Coal and Steel Community and Euratom matters should draw guidance from these provisions (which will be contained in the EC Treaty only). This Declaration also covers action against fraud — see paragraph 14.10 below.

Documents originating in Member States

13.19   In a further Declaration, the Member States state that the principles to be established will allow a Member State to ask the Council or the Commission not to give out a document originating from that Member State without its prior agreement.

Quality of Legislation

13.20   In a Declaration the Member States emphasise that the quality of the drafting of Community legislation is crucial if it is to be properly implemented by national authorities and better understood by the public and business circles. In order to help to achieve this, the European Parliament, the Council and the Commission ought to lay down agreed guidelines and speed up the codification of legislative texts so that they will be more accessible to the public.

CHAPTER 14

Other Community Policies

14.1   Changes have also been made in relation to a number of other Community policies. These are outlined below:

Citizenship of the Union

14.2   Two changes have been made to the section of the EC Treaty dealing with citizenship of the Union.

Clarification of concept of EU citizenship

14.3   **First,** the concept as it appears in the EC Treaty has been clarified. Article 8 which establishes citizenship of the Union already provides that every person holding the nationality of a Member State shall be a citizen of the Union. While it was clearly implied in this provision that citizenship of the Union would be complementary to national citizenship, it was agreed in the negotiations that it would be desirable to remove any possible doubt by making this explicit in the Treaty. Accordingly a sentence has been added to the Article stating that *"citizenship of the Union shall complement and not replace national citizenship"*.

Right to correspond in a Treaty language

14.4   **Second,** a new provision has been added to one of the Articles on citizenship (8d) providing that any citizen of the Union may write to any of the institutions or bodies of the Union in any one of the twelve Treaty languages and may expect that any answer will be in the same language. This new provision was of significance to Belgium, where language issues are a matter of some sensitivity. It is also of significance to Ireland. It will allow Irish people, or indeed any citizen of the Union who may wish to do so, to correspond with the Community institutions in the Irish language.

Position of the Irish language

14.5   Irish is not recognised in the relevant Regulation as an official or a working language of the Community but it is one of the twelve "Treaty languages", as they may be called, which are listed in Article 248 of the EC Treaty. This means that each successive Treaty is published in Irish as well as in the eleven other languages and the texts in Irish are equally authentic and have equal status with those in all other languages. The new Treaty provision, by saying that every citizen of the Union may write to any of the institutions or bodies in one of the languages mentioned in Article 248 of the EC Treaty and have an answer in the same language, in effect establishes a right for any citizen to correspond with the Community institutions and bodies in Irish.

Education

14.6   The new Treaty will add a paragraph stressing the importance of education to the Preamble of the EC Treaty. It reads as follows:

"Determined to promote the development of the highest possible level of knowledge for their peoples through a wide access to education and through its continuous updating."

Culture

14.7   Title IX of the EC Treaty, comprising a single Article 128, deals with culture. Paragraph 4 of this Article, as it stands, stipulates that *"the Community shall take cultural aspects into account in its action under other provisions of this Treaty"*. The new Treaty will add a phrase referring to cultural diversity so that the paragraph will read as follows: *"The Community shall take cultural aspects into account in its action under other provisions of this Treaty, in particular in order to respect and to promote the diversity of its cultures"*.

Sport

14.8   In a Declaration, the Member States emphasise the social significance of sport and its role in bringing people together. Accordingly they call on European Union bodies to listen to sports associations when issues affecting sport are at stake and to give special consideration to the particular characteristics of amateur sport.

Fraud affecting the financial interests of the Community

14.9   There is already a provision in the EC Treaty (Article 209a) which obliges Member States to take the same measures to counter fraud affecting the financial interests of the Community as they take to counter fraud affecting their own financial interests. The new Treaty will strengthen this provision and extend it to any other illegal activities affecting the financial interests of the Community. It will also create an obligation on the Council, acting in co-decision with the Parliament, and after consulting the Court of Auditors, to adopt the necessary measures in relation to preventing and fighting fraud affecting the financial interests of the Community. The aim will be to afford "effective and equivalent protection in the Member States". These measures, however, are not to relate to the application of national criminal law or the national administration of justice. This will provide a new legal basis for Council action in this respect.

14.10   In a Declaration, the Member States also expressed the view that the European Parliament, the Council and the Commission, when acting in European Coal and Steel Community and Euratom matters, should draw guidance from these new provisions (which will be contained in the EC Treaty only). This Declaration also covers transparency and access to documents — see paragraph 13.18 above.

Customs cooperation

14.11   The new Treaty will add a new Article (116) to the EC Treaty which will provide that the Council, acting in co-decision with the European Parliament, shall take measures to strengthen customs cooperation between Member States and between Member States and the Commission. These measures, however, are not to relate to the application of national criminal law or the national administration of justice.

Outermost regions

14.12   The new Treaty will also strengthen the Article in the EC Treaty (Article 227(2)) which provides for special consideration for the French overseas Departments, the Portuguese territories of the Azores and Madeira and the Spanish territories of the Canary Islands.

14.13   The amended article will now provide a legal basis for action by the Council, acting by qualified majority, on a proposal from the Commission and after consulting the European Parliament, to adopt specific measures laying down the conditions of application of the Treaty, including common policies, to these regions.

14.14   These measures will take account of the specific character of these regions, including their remoteness, insularity, small size and general dependence on a few products. Account is also to be taken of such matters as customs and trade policies, fiscal policy, free zones, agriculture and fisheries policies, State aids and conditions of access to structural funds. The Council is to adopt the measures referred to, which will take into account the special characteristics and constraints applying to these *"outermost regions"*, without undermining the integrity and coherence of the Community legal order, including the internal market and common policies.

Island Regions

14.15   The Community is already required (Article 130a) to aim at reducing disparities between the levels of development of the various regions and reducing the backwardness of the least favoured regions including rural areas. The new Treaty will add a reference to *"islands"* to this provision. In a Declaration, Member States recognise that island regions suffer from structural handicaps. It states that Community legislation must take account of this and specific measures may be taken, where justified, to integrate these regions better into the internal market on fair conditions.

Overseas countries and territories

14.16   Special arrangements are provided in Article 131 of the EC Treaty to associate with the Community the non-European countries and territories which are dependencies of certain Member States. The aim was to promote their economic and social development and to establish close economic relations between them and the Community as a whole. The number of such territories has greatly shrunk and today there are only twenty extremely scattered island territories with a total population of about 900,000.

14.17   In a Declaration, the Member States invite the Council to review the association agreements with these territories by February 2000 with a view to promoting more effectively their economic and social development, developing their economic relations with the EU, taking account of their diversity and improving the effectiveness of the financial instrument.

Services of general economic interest

14.18 During the negotiations which led to the new Treaty there was some debate on the question of how far bodies such as utilities which are required to provide public services on an equal footing throughout a Member State, even in areas of low population, should receive special consideration in the operation of the Treaty provisions including those in relation to state aids. France in particular pressed this issue, while making the point that it did not want to distinguish between public sector and private enterprise bodies providing what were called *"services of general economic interest."* Other Member States, however, feared that the effect could be to free public sector enterprises entirely from constraints in the matter of state aids.

14.19 A compromise was reached and the new Treaty will include a new Article 7d in the EC Treaty. This will provide that, without prejudice to the Articles dealing with state aids, and given the particular place within the Union occupied by such services, the Community and the Member States *"shall take care that such services operate on the basis of principles and conditions which enable them to fulfil their mission"*.

Declaration

14.20 As part of the compromise between the two positions it was agreed by the Member States to make a Declaration which says that these provisions are to be implemented *"with full respect for the jurisprudence of the Court of Justice"*. This will include taking account of the principles of equality of treatment, quality and continuity of such services.

Public Service Broadcasting

14.21 During the course of the negotiations which led to the new Treaty a substantial number of Member States expressed concern that judgments to be given in cases pending before the Court of Justice could in practice undermine the right of Member States to provide for the funding of public service broadcasting. A Protocol has accordingly been added to the EC Treaty on this question.

14.22   The Protocol is a careful balance between the large number of Member States whose principal concern was that Member States should be allowed to continue to fund public service broadcasting (even if the Court should rule otherwise under the existing Treaty) and should be able themselves to define the public service remit; and those who were concerned about the possibility that this could create unfair competition for commercial broadcasting.

14.23   The Protocol takes into consideration *"that the system of public broadcasting in the Member States is directly related to the democratic, social and cultural needs of each society and to the need to preserve media pluralism"*. It sets out interpretative provisions the effect of which will be to permit Member States to provide for the funding of public service broadcasting insofar as such funding is granted for *"the fulfillment of the public service remit as conferred, defined and organised by each Member State"*; and that such funding does not affect competition and trading conditions in the Community to an extent which would be contrary to the common interest.

Public Credit Institutions in Germany

14.24   A Declaration by the Member States takes account of a particular situation which obtains in Germany where local authorities are involved in public credit institutions. In effect the Declaration recognises that the way in which Germany enables local authorities to run such bodies is a matter for Germany itself to decide at national level. It recalls that the European Council has invited the Commission to apply the same standards where similar cases exist in other Member States.

14.25   Austria and Luxembourg have joined in adding a Declaration expressing the view that the Declaration in relation to public credit institutions in Germany applies also to similar institutions in their countries.

Voluntary Service activities

14.26   A Declaration made by the Member States recognises the important contribution made by voluntary services to developing social solidarity. It states that the Community will encourage the European dimension of such bodies with emphasis on the exchange of information and experiences and on the participation of the young and of the elderly in voluntary work.

Animal Welfare

14.27   There is already a Declaration, made at the time of the Maastricht Treaty in 1992, in which Member States call on the European Parliament, the Council and the Commission, as well as the Member States themselves, to pay full regard to the welfare requirements of animals in Community legislation on the common agricultural policy, transport, the internal market and research. The new Treaty will modify and qualify the content of this Declaration to some extent and at the same time give it the new and higher legal status of a Protocol to the EC Treaty.

14.28   This Protocol provides that the Community and the Member States shall pay full regard in such legislation to the welfare requirements of animals *"while respecting the legislative or administrative provisions and customs of the Member States relating in particular to religious rites, cultural traditions and regional heritage."*

Trans-European Networks

14.29   The new Treaty will amend the provisions in Title XII of the EC Treaty which deal with support by the Community for the development of Trans-European Networks (TENs) in transport, telecommunications, and energy infrastructures.

14.30   At present the text of Article 129c permits the Community to *"support the financial efforts made by the Member States for projects of common interest financed by Member States..."* The new text will broaden this so that it allows the Community to *"support projects of common interest supported by Member States..."* (emphasis added). The aim of this amendment is to permit Community support to be given to projects even if they are not receiving finance from Member State Governments.

Statistics

14.31   The Treaties at present do not provide any explicit legal basis for the collection and production of statistics. The new Treaty will insert a new Article in the EC Treaty to provide such a basis.

14.32 The new Article 213a provides that the Council, acting in co-decision with the Parliament (which will involve qualified majority voting in the Council), is to adopt measures for the production of statistics where necessary for the activities of the Community. Certain standards are to govern the production of Community statistics: impartiality, reliability, objectivity, scientific independence, cost-effectiveness and statistical confidentiality. The production of such statistics is not to "*entail excessive burdens on economic operators*".

CHAPTER FIFTEEN

The External Relations of the Union

The Common Foreign and Security Policy

Background

15.1   From the early 1970s onwards the Member States coordinated their positions on foreign policy matters in European Political Cooperation (EPC). This was a separate framework of inter-governmental cooperation which was developed alongside the supra-national structure of the Community.

15.2   In the Single European Act of 1986 the Member States entered into a more formal Treaty commitment. In Title III they committed themselves to coordinate their positions more closely on *"the political and economic aspects of security"*.

15.3   Six years later these provisions in turn were further developed and restructured as the Common Foreign and Security Policy (CFSP) of the European Union in the Maastricht Treaty of 1992. The CFSP is now commonly referred to as the Second Pillar of the Union.

The present position

15.4   The provisions governing the Common Foreign and Security Policy (CFSP) are set out in Title V of the EU (Maastricht) Treaty. While these provisions involve commitments and Treaty obligations for the Member States within the Union, the cooperation remains substantially inter-governmental in character. Decisions are taken by unanimity, subject only to the possibility that Member States by unanimity might decide that measures implementing "joint actions" could be adopted by a qualified majority.

15.5   The CFSP section of the Maastricht Treaty begins by setting objectives. They include safeguarding the common values, fundamental interests and independence of the Union and strengthening the security of the Union and its Member States in all ways; preserving peace and strengthening international security in accordance with the UN Charter, the Helsinki Final Act and the

Paris Charter; promoting international cooperation; and developing and consolidating democracy and the rule of law and respect for human rights.

15.6 Two types of legal instrument are provided for: (a) common positions to which national policies are expected to conform and (b) joint actions which apply in defined areas of foreign policy and are intended to be binding in their effect.

15.7 The Maastricht Treaty provides that the CFSP *"shall include all questions related to the security of the Union, including the eventual framing of a common defence policy which might in time lead to a common defence"*. It also describes the Western European Union (WEU) as *"an integral part of the development of the Union"*. The Union is to request the WEU *"to elaborate and implement decisions and actions of the Union which have defence implications"*.

15.8 The Article dealing with these issues (J.4) includes a paragraph which, although indirectly expressed, was intended to take account of the particular position of Ireland as a non-member of military alliances and also of the EU Member States which are also members of NATO. It provides that *"the policy of the Union..shall not prejudice the specific character of the security and defence policy of certain Member States"*; and also that it shall *"respect the obligations of certain Member States under the North Atlantic Alliance and be compatible with the common security and defence policy established within that framework."*

15.9 The Maastricht Treaty also envisaged that there would be an Intergovernmental Conference at which the provisions of this article could be revised on the basis of a report by the Council to the European Council in 1996.

15.10 The European Parliament has a role under the CFSP but it is more limited than under the First Pillar. The Parliament is to be consulted on *"the main aspects and the basic choices"* of the CFSP; it is to be kept regularly informed by the Presidency and the Commission; it may ask questions of the Council or make recommendations to it; and it holds an annual debate. The Court of Justice does not have jurisdiction in relation to the CFSP.

Reasons for change

15.11 The Maastricht Treaty established the CFSP at a time of profound and rapid change in international life as the Cold War came to an end in the early 1990s. But while the threat of East/West conflict leading to global war has receded, conflicts in former Yugoslavia, in parts of the former Soviet Union, and in a number of areas in Africa were evidence of a new instability in international affairs.

15.12   Against this background, it was a widely held view among the Member States that the review which was provided for in the Maastricht Treaty in 1992 should seek to make the Foreign and Security Policy of the Union more effective, more coherent, and more visible. They wanted it to reflect the importance of the European Union on the international scene and the concern of its citizens that the Union should make a contribution to international peace and security commensurate with its economic capacity.

What the new Treaty will do

Outline

15.13   The new Treaty will make substantial amendments to the existing provisions governing the CFSP as established under the Maastricht Treaty of 1992. The main effects of the new Treaty, in summary, will be that:

  (i) the decision-making procedures will be revised somewhat: a greater use of qualified majority voting in some respects is envisaged but it will remain possible for a Member State in the last resort to block a decision;

 (ii) the wording of the security/defence provisions will also be revised somewhat; the reference to a common defence is expressed as a possibility but not as an agreed objective;

(iii) specific provision is made for the carrying out of what have come to be called the Petersberg tasks. These are humanitarian and rescue tasks, peacekeeping tasks and tasks of combat forces in crisis management including peacemaking. They will be carried out by the WEU at the initiative of the Union; participation will be open to all Member States of the Union but will not be obligatory;

 (iv) operational expenditure arising from implementation of the CFSP will now, in the ordinary course, be carried on the Community budget unless Member States, by unanimity, decide otherwise;

  (v) the Secretary General of the Council will now become "High Representative for the CFSP". He/she will help the Council by contributing to the formulation and implementation of policy and, at the request of the Presidency, may conduct political dialogue with other countries and organisations on behalf of the Council.

The provisions of the new Treaty are explained in greater detail below.

Objectives

15.14   The objectives of the CFSP as set out in the Maastricht Treaty (see paragraph 15.5 above) include safeguarding "*the common values, fundamental interests and independence of the Union.*" This objective will be re-phrased; references to the integrity of the Union and to the United Nations Charter will be added; and the reference to Member States will be dropped. As revised, the objective will now read "*to safeguard the common values, fundamental interests, and integrity of the Union in conformity with the principles of the United Nations Charter.*"

15.15   Another objective set in the Maastricht Treaty was "*to preserve peace and strengthen international security in accordance with the principles of the United Nations Charter, as well as the principles of the Helsinki Final Act and the objectives of the Paris Charter*". The phrase "*including those on external borders*" has been added here at the end of this objective. The Helsinki Final Act, signed in 1975, already commits all OSCE Members, including all Member States of the Union, to a number of principles guiding relations between them, including principles on the changing of frontiers peacefully and by agreement and on the inviolability of frontiers.

Decision-making

15.16   The nature and structure of decision-making under the CFSP will be revised and systematised to a somewhat greater extent under the new Treaty. The role of the European Council in defining principles and general guidelines, which was already provided for in the Maastricht Treaty, will also be highlighted to a greater extent and it will be made explicit that it will now include matters with defence implications. (How these will be dealt with is explained further below).

15.17   Under the new provisions the European Council, will decide on "*common strategies*" in selected areas where the Member States have important interests in common, and the (General Affairs) Council will recommend and implement such strategies. As under the existing Treaty, the Council will continue to adopt joint actions, which are to be binding, and common positions. The provisions governing these two types of legal instrument have been clarified somewhat although their essentials will not change.

15.18   The procedure for taking decisions under the CFSP will, however, be revised. The principle that decisions under the CFSP should be taken by unanimity, as is appropriate to inter-governmental cooperation, is still retained but it will be modified in a number of ways.

Abstentions

15.19   In the first place it is made explicit that abstentions shall not prevent unanimity.

Constructive abstention

15.20   Secondly, a new provision for what could be called "*constructive abstention*" has been added (This term is not used in the Treaty). This will allow a Member State when a proposal is being adopted to make a formal declaration. The effect will be that the Member State concerned permits the proposal to be adopted and accepts it as a decision committing the Union but that it will not itself be bound to apply it. If, however, the number of Member States seeking to avail of this "opt-out" provision for constructive abstention amounts to more than one third of the weighted votes, the proposal is not adopted.

Provision for qualified majority voting with exceptions

15.21   Thirdly, and by way of exception to the general rule of unanimity, the Council will, normally, act by qualified majority in two cases:

(a) when taking a decision on the basis of a common strategy already adopted by the European Council;

(b) when adopting any decision implementing a joint action or a common position.

15.22   This provision for the use of qualified majority voting in certain circumstances will itself, however, be subject to two qualifications:

(a) qualified majority voting will not apply to decisions having military or defence implications. Such decisions will continue to be taken by unanimity. "Constructive abstention" as explained in paragraph 15.20 above may be availed of.

(b) voting by qualified majority will be subject to what has been described loosely as "an emergency brake" procedure.

15.23   The so-called "emergency brake" procedure means that if a Member State declares in the Council that "*for important and stated reasons of national policy*" it intends to oppose a decision to be taken by qualified majority, then no vote is to be taken. Thus the proposal is not adopted. However, if a qualified majority in the Council wish to pursue the matter further then the issue is referred to the European Council. The final decision will thus rest at Head of State or Government level where decisions are taken by unanimity.

15.24   The net effect of this provision is that a Member State which is strongly opposed to a decision which would otherwise be taken by qualified majority may block it in the last analysis but in order to do so may need to maintain its opposition at Summit level.

New role for Secretary General of the Council

15.25   The new Treaty will give the Secretary General of the Council new functions as *"High Representative for the Common Foreign and Security Policy"*. In that capacity he/she will assist the Council by contributing to the formulation, preparation and implementation of policy decisions in the CFSP area. The "High Representative may also be assigned a representational role on behalf of the Council at the request of the Presidency.

Revision of the arrangements for the representation of the Union

15.26   The Maastricht Treaty assigns to the Presidency the role of representing the Union on CFSP matters. It also provides for an arrangement, which has been commonly called "the troika" and which is designed to help the Presidency, in particular, in its representational role on behalf of the Union. This allows the Presidency to be assisted, if need be, by both the previous and immediately following Presidencies. The new Treaty will revise these arrangements somewhat. The reference to the immediately preceding Presidency will be dropped but the reference to the immediately following Presidency will be retained in order to ensure continuity.

15.27   The net effect of these provisions is to restructure the representational arrangements. The Presidency will continue to speak for the Union and may be assisted, if need be, by the Member State which is due to take over the Presidency immediately after it. The Commission, as at present, will continue to be fully associated with the Presidency in these tasks. The Secretary-General of the Council as High Representative for the Common Foreign and Security Policy will assist the Presidency.

International agreements

15.28   There will be a new provision establishing the procedure to apply where it is necessary to conclude international agreements in implementation of the provisions of the Treaty with other states outside the Union or with international organisations (This provision will also apply to international agreements in relation to Police and Judicial Cooperation matters arising under the Third Pillar — see paragraph 8.45 above).

15.29   Under the new procedure the Council, by unanimity, may authorise the Presidency, assisted by the Commission as appropriate, to open negotiations. At the end of the negotiations, the agreements are to be concluded by unanimous decision of the Council, on a recommendation from the Presidency. This means that, in principle, individual ratification by Member States will not be necessary but the new Treaty will provide that no agreement shall be binding on a Member State if its representative in the Council states that it has to comply with the requirements of its own constitutional procedure before it takes effect. The other Member States may agree in that case that the agreement should apply provisionally to them.

15.30   A Declaration made by the Member States referring to this provision states that any agreements concluded in this way will not imply any transfer of competence from Member States to the Union.

Budgetary issues

15.31   The new Treaty will also involve some revision of the budgetary provisions. Under the present Treaty, administrative expenditure arising under the CFSP is met from the Community budget. Operational expenditure in implementing decisions is normally a matter for the Member States but it may also be decided by unanimity to charge it to the Community budget.

15.32   The new Treaty will change this situation. Operational expenditure on implementation of decisions will now also be charged to the Community budget, except for expenditure arising from operations having military or defence implications and cases where the Council by unanimity decides otherwise.

15.33   In cases where such expenditure is not charged to the Community budget it will be charged to Member States in accordance with a GNP scale, unless the Council, by unanimity, decides on some other arrangement. However, Member States which have availed of the "constructive abstention" provision described above will not be obliged to contribute to the cost of implementing a decision with military or defence implications.

Inter-Institutional Agreement with the Parliament

15.34   Although it is not formally a part of the Treaty, the Member States have also reached agreement with the European Parliament and the Commission in regard to the financing of the CFSP. This Inter-Institutional Agreement provides that expenditure under the CFSP shall be treated as "non-compulsory expenditure". This means in practice that the Parliament will have a greater say in relation to it. Other provisions of the agreement allow greater latitude for transfer between budget headings and provide for a concertation procedure between the Council and the Parliament.

15.35   The net effect of the agreement, taken as a whole, is to establish agreed rules under which the Parliament will have something closer to a joint role with the Council in budgetary decisions relating to CFSP expenditure; and the Presidency will consult the Parliament annually on a document established by the Council on the main aspects of the CFSP, including the financial implications for the Community budget.

Policy Planning and Early Warning Unit

15.36   In a Declaration, the Member States have also agreed that a Policy Planning and Early Warning Unit is to be established in the General Secretariat of the Council under the responsibility of the Secretary General who is now to be described formally as *"the High Representative for the Common Foreign and Security Policy"*. The main tasks of the Unit will be monitoring and analysing foreign policy developments, providing assessments and early warning reports and producing *"argued policy options papers"* to be presented under the responsibility of the Presidency as a contribution to policy formulation in the Council. The Unit will include personnel drawn from the General Secretariat of the Council, from the Member States, from the Commission and from the WEU.

Security and Defence issues

15.37   The new Treaty will also revise the provisions of the Common Foreign and Security Policy bearing on security and defence issues. These changes are described further below.

Background

15.38   The Single European Act of 1986 provided for coordination between Member States on *"the political and economic aspects of security"*. The Maastricht Treaty in 1992 provided that the Common Foreign and Security Policy of the Union which it established should include *"all questions related to the security of the Union, including the eventual framing of a common defence policy, which might in time lead to a common defence"*. The Maastricht Treaty described the WEU (the Western European Union) as *"an integral part of the development of the Union"*; and it provided that the Union would request the WEU to implement decisions having military or defence implications.

15.39   The Maastricht Treaty also contained a paragraph which was inserted to take account of the particular position of Ireland as a non-member of military alliances (*"the policy of the Union in accordance with this Article shall not prejudice the specific character of the security and defence policy of certain Member States"*) and which also required that the obligations under the North Atlantic Treaty of those EU Member States which were also members of NATO should be respected (see below).

What the new Treaty will do

15.40   The new Treaty will revise these provisions in four main ways which are closely inter-linked. Some other provisions, including that mentioned in the preceding paragraph, will be retained.

15.41   **First,** the language in relation to a future defence policy will be changed. The Maastricht Treaty provided that the CFSP was to include *"all questions related to the security of the Union, including the eventual framing of a common defence policy, which might in time lead to a common defence"*. The new Treaty says that the CFSP *"shall include all questions relating to the security of the Union, including the progressive framing of a common defence policy in accordance with the second sub-paragraph, which might lead to a common defence, should the European Council so decide. It shall in that case recommend to the Member States the adoption of such a decision in accordance with their respective constitutional requirements."*

15.42   The *"second sub-paragraph"*, which is mentioned in this new text deals with the EU/WEU relationship. By this linkage the text, in effect, is saying that *"the progressive framing of a common defence policy"* which it looks to would be structured around a further development of the EU/WEU relationship, which was established in the Maastricht Treaty and which is taken a stage further by the new Treaty.

EU/WEU relationship

15.43   **Second,** and linked with this, the provisions in regard to EU/WEU relations have been revised somewhat. The WEU was described in the Maastricht Treaty as *"an integral part of the development of the Union"* and the Union was to request it *"to elaborate and implement decisions and actions of the Union which have defence implications"*. The new Treaty repeats the description of the WEU as *"an integral part of the development of the Union"* and adds that it provides the Union *"with access to an operational capability, notably in the context of paragraph 2"* (Paragraph 2 is the paragraph which deals with the "Petersberg tasks" — see paragraph 15.51 below)

15.44   **Third,** the possibility of a future merger of the two organisations is evoked. The new Treaty text says that the Union is to *"foster closer institutional relations with the WEU with a view to the possibility of the integration of the WEU into the Union, should the European Council so decide. It shall in that case recommend to the Member States the adoption of such a decision in accordance with their respective constitutional requirements."*

15.45   The wording used here reflects a continuing lack of agreement between Member States on this issue. During the negotiation of the new Treaty some

Member States proposed a draft Protocol which would have explicitly established the integration of the WEU into the EU as an aim and set out three stages through which it was to be realised. That proposal was not adopted: it was opposed on the one hand by some Member States, including Ireland, who are not members of military alliances; and, from a different perspective, by other Member States who rely on NATO and were concerned about anything that might blur its role as their main defence bulwark.

15.46   The phrase about the "*possibility*" of integration was agreed as a compromise between those who wanted such a Protocol and those who were opposed. The Member States which, like Ireland, had difficulty with the idea of a Protocol providing for future integration, were able to accept this text because it is phrased in terms of "*possibility*" rather than as an agreed objective, and qualified further by the references to the several levels of decision-making which would be necessary.

15.47   At the first stage, according to the provision in the new Treaty, such a decision, like the decision on a common defence mentioned above to which in practice it would be linked, would be considered by the European Council. In the European Council, which brings together the Heads of State or Government of the Member States and the President of the Commission, assisted by the Foreign Ministers and a member of the Commission, all decisions are taken by unanimity.

15.48   If the European Council were to take any such decision and recommend it to the Member States for adoption "*in accordance with their respective constitutional requirements*", it would then be for each Member State to decide whether or not to adopt the decision(s); and, if so, what constitutional requirements would arise.

15.49   This means that if such a decision were taken by the European Council then it would be for Ireland, as for the other Member States, to decide on its adoption in accordance with its particular constitutional requirements. The Government, like the two previous Governments, have stated that, whether or not such a decision would require an amendment to the Constitution, it would be put to the people for decision in a referendum.

15.50   A further level of decision making would be necessary if any future decision to move to a common EU defence were to be carried through in practice by the integration of the WEU into the EU, as the Member States who proposed the draft Protocol had envisaged. Such a merger of two organisations with different obligations and commitments and, indeed, different though partially overlapping membership, would require major Treaty revision on the part of both. In the EU it would require the convening of a new Intergovernmental

Conference where proposals made to amend the Treaties would require unanimity for adoption. Any revised Treaty which might be agreed would then have to be submitted for national ratification by each Member State in accordance with its constitutional requirements.

The "Petersberg tasks"

15.51   **Fourth**, the new Treaty will bring the Petersberg tasks within the scope of the European Union for the first time. This is done by stating that questions dealt with in the Article relating to security aspects of the CFSP are to include *"humanitarian and rescue tasks, peacekeeping tasks and tasks of combat forces in crisis management, including peacemaking"*. (This is what the phrase "notably in the context of paragraph 2" mentioned at paragraph 15.43 above refers to.)

15.52   The Petersberg tasks are so called after the conference centre near Bonn where a declaration which embodied them was adopted in 1992. They were elaborated against the background of the great changes which were taking place in European security following the end of the Cold War. They provide a framework within which the WEU can provide effective support (including through calling on NATO resources such as, for example, airlift capacity, infrastructure and communications) for implementation of measures for conflict prevention and crisis management, including peacekeeping activities decided on by the UN Security Council or by the OSCE (Organisation for Security and Cooperation in Europe).

15.53   The new Treaty states that the EU will avail itself of the WEU to elaborate and implement decisions and actions which have defence implications. In particular, it envisages that the EU will avail itself of the WEU to elaborate and implement EU decisions on the Petersberg tasks which are now brought within the scope of the CFSP. When it does so, all Member States will be entitled to participate fully in the tasks in question. This is an entitlement – there will be no obligation on any Member State to take part. The practical arrangements to be made between the Council and the WEU will be such as to allow all Member States which do take part in one of these tasks to take part also fully and on an equal footing in planning and decision-taking in the WEU.

15.54   Since the new Treaty envisages that the EU will be availing itself in this way of the WEU to carry through decisions on Petersberg tasks, which may be made within the scope of the CFSP, it was necessary to consider how the practical arrangements would operate. A Protocol attached to the new Treaty provides that, within a year after it enters into force, the Union, together with the WEU, is to draw up arrangements for enhanced cooperation between the two organisations; and in a Declaration the Member States invite the Council to seek early adoption of appropriate arrangements for security clearance of personnel of the General Secretariat of the Council. In a procedure similar to that followed in relation to the Maastricht Treaty, the WEU adopted its own Declaration which took note of the security/defence provisions of the Amsterdam Treaty. The EU Intergovernmental Conference in a Declaration to the Final Act then took note in turn of this WEU Declaration.

The security and defence policy of certain Member States

15.55   As noted in paragraph 15.40 above, some provisions of the Maastricht Treaty in this whole area will not be changed. In particular, the new Treaty will retain the provision which was inserted to take account of Ireland's particular policy of military neutrality on the one hand, and the position of the NATO members of the Union on the other. The Treaty will thus continue to provide, in an implied reference to Ireland (and now also to other European Union Member States who are militarily neutral) that *"the policy of the Union in accordance with this Article shall not prejudice the specific character of the security and defence policy of certain Member States..."*

Optional cooperation on armaments

15.56   During the negotiations, some Member States wished also to develop the opportunities for cooperation on armaments under the EU and EC Treaties. The compromise which was agreed is the inclusion in the new Treaty of a provision which will allow Member States, to the extent that they so wish, to cooperate in the matter of armaments. The text reads *"the progressive framing of a common defence policy will be supported, as Member States consider appropriate, by cooperation between them in the field of armaments"*.

Future review

15.57   All of the foregoing provisions relating to the security aspects of the CFSP are contained in a single Article (J7) of the new Treaty. The last paragraph of that Article provides that it is to be the subject of a future review. This would require that another Inter-governmental Conference be convened at some time in the future to consider any further Treaty amendments which might be proposed. However, the new Treaty does not set any date or envisage any timeframe for such a review.

External Economic Relations

Background

15.58   The environment in which international economic negotiations take place has changed radically in recent years. The focus was previously on trade

121

in goods but now new areas such as services, direct foreign investment and intellectual property are of great importance. The question of how best to provide the Community with the capacity to conduct effective multilateral negotiations in this new and changing environment, and particularly in the global system established through the World Trade Organisation (the successor to the GATT), was the subject of considerable debate in the negotiations which led to the new Treaty.

15.59　The present Treaty provides (Article 113) that when agreements with other states or international organisations need to be negotiated the Council will authorise the Commission to open the necessary negotiations. The Commission is to conduct these negotiations in consultation with a special committee appointed by the Council (the so-called "113 Committee") and within the framework set by the Council.

15.60　At the close of the negotiations, the agreement is to be concluded by the Council on a proposal from the Commission (Article 228). In authorising the opening of negotiations and in concluding the agreement the Council is to act by qualified majority vote on the basis of a Commission proposal but unanimity is required for matters where unanimity applies for internal rules within the Community and also for association agreements.

15.61　The significance of these provisions is that the negotiations are conducted by the Commission within a mandate given by the Council; that the agreements, on being concluded by the Council, need not be referred back to Member States for individual ratification; and that decisions for the most part, are taken by qualified majority vote.

Effect of recent case-law of the Court

15.62　In recent case-law, however, the Court of Justice has confirmed that, as a rule, these provisions of the existing Treaty, although they apply to trade in goods, do not apply to negotiations in regard to services, intellectual property and direct foreign investment.

15.63　The result, in the view of many Member States and of the Commission, is that the Community does not have the capacity which it needs to cope with the changing international economic environment and that it is inhibited in negotiation on issues which are now of central importance. During the negotiation of the new Treaty there were, however, objections by some Member States to extending the competence of the Community to negotiations on these new areas; and there were also evident sensitivities on the part of several Member States who felt they had not been adequately consulted by the Commission in some recent international economic negotiations. This made it more difficult to secure agreement on amendments to the Treaty which would, among other things, extend the role of the Commission in conducting such negotiations.

What the new Treaty will do

15.64   In the event the new Treaty does not itself extend the application of the existing Treaty provisions to the newly important areas of services, intellectual property and foreign direct investment. It does, however, add a new provision to Article 113 which will allow the Council, by unanimity, on a proposal from the Commission and after consulting the Parliament to extend the application of those provisions to international negotiations and agreements on services and intellectual property.

Provisional application of agreements

15.65   A further amendment will be made to the provisions of the EC Treaty (Article 228.2) which set out the procedure for the conclusion of agreements by the Council. The effect of the changes will be to allow the signing of an agreement to be accompanied by a decision on provisional application before it enters into force.

Suspension of agreements

15.66   The Article as amended will also provide that a similar procedure is to apply to a decision to suspend the application of an international agreement and a decision on the positions to be adopted by the Community in bodies set up under association agreements, the decisions of which have legal effects — except for decisions which change the institutional framework of the agreement.

15.67   When an agreement is suspended or applied provisionally in this way the European Parliament is to be informed fully and immediately. It is also to be informed of the establishment of the Community position in bodies established under association agreements.

CHAPTER SIXTEEN

Institutions

Background — general survey of the main issues

16.1 In the negotiations which led up to the new Treaty all Member States saw it as important to ensure that the institutions of the Union should function effectively, both now and in a future enlarged Union; and that they be seen to be more open and democratic in their operation. There was a particular focus on making decision-making in the Council more effective; on the size and structure of the Commission; and on giving the European Parliament a larger role so as to make it truly a "co-legislator" with the Council.

16.2 Of these, the most difficult issues to resolve proved to be the system of voting in the Council and the size of the Commission. There was a greater readiness on the part of Member States to extend the "co-decision" procedure involving the Parliament to new areas and to make its operation somewhat simpler.

16.3 The way in which the new Treaty deals with these issues is explained further below. The Treaty also makes changes of relevance to other Community institutions and bodies- notably the Court of Justice, the Court of Auditors, the Economic and Social Committee and the Committee of the Regions. These are also explained below. Before dealing with the changes, however, it may be helpful to outline some of the issues which arose in the negotiation of the new Treaty.

Decision-making in the Council

16.4 Two main issues arose under this heading:

  (i) the extension to new areas of the system of qualified majority voting;

  (ii) the weighting of votes in the Council as between larger and smaller Member States.

Qualified majority voting in the Council

16.5 For decisions on some issues the Treaties stipulate that there must be unanimity while for others they provide for decision by qualified majority vote. In a qualified majority vote (often referred to as qmv), the votes of Member

States are assigned different weights according to a scale set out in the EC Treaty (Article 148.2)

16.6 The four largest Member States (Germany, the UK, France and Italy) have 10 votes each; Spain 8 ; Belgium, Greece, Netherlands and Portugal 5 each; Austria and Sweden 4 each; Denmark, Finland and Ireland 3 each; and Luxembourg has 2. If a decision to be taken in the Council by a qualified majority is based on a Commission proposal then a total of at least 62 votes is required for adoption; qualified majority decisions other than those based on Commission proposals require in addition that the necessary 62 votes be cast by at least 10 Member States.

16.7 Since 1973, when Ireland, the UK and Denmark joined, the number of Member States has increased — first from nine to ten, then to twelve and now to fifteen. The Union is now preparing to open negotiations with a number of other countries which have applied to join. On the assumption that these negotiations are successful, the membership will expand again over the coming years.

16.8 A larger membership clearly makes decision-making in the Council more difficult in areas where unanimity is required since this means in practice that every Member State has a veto. From one viewpoint a Member State may see this as an advantage because it can block a proposal which it opposes. But it may also prove a disadvantage because another Member State may veto a proposal on some other issue which it wanted to see adopted .

16.9 Under the Treaties, qualified majority voting already applies in many areas. During the negotiations leading to the new Treaty many Member States agreed in principle that amending the Treaties to provide for a further extension of the areas for use of qualified majority voting, instead of unanimity, could help to avert the danger of blockage in decision-making as the membership of the Union increases. They also knew that, since any Treaty change must be agreed by all. it would be easier to make the necessary changes now rather than later when the membership has grown further. Nevertheless, when it came to detailed decisions on specific areas where qualified majority voting rather than unanimity should be made the rule there was often a reluctance on the part of one or other Member State to agree to change and unanimity was thus difficult to achieve.

Voting weights in the Council

16.10 A second aspect of the work of the Council which became a focus for much discussion was the wish of some larger Member States to change the

125

present weighting of votes as set out in the Treaty; and possibly also, the thresholds (in the sense of the number of votes necessary for adoption or rejection of a proposal).

16.11   Some of these larger Member States argued that on a population basis there is already a considerable disproportion in voting weights between the larger and the smaller Member States; and that this will increase with the likely admission to the Union of other smaller or middle-sized states. Some also were willing to agree to a substantially greater use of qualified majority voting only if this had as counterpart a change in voting weights in favour of larger Member States so as to give greater importance to population. Yet another view was that, conversely, a change in voting weights should not be considered unless there were agreement on a substantial extension of qualified majority voting.

16.12   The alternative possibility of giving greater weight to population by introducing a "dual majority" requirement rather than by changing voting "weights" was also discussed. This could mean, for example, adding an additional requirement for adoption of a proposal: it would be necessary not only that it receive a certain total of weighted votes but also that the votes in favour should be cast by Member States representing a certain percentage of the total population of the Union.

16.13   Smaller Member States on the other hand argued that relative population size is only one factor in the weighting of votes in the Council — the Treaty must also take account of the fact that each Member State, regardless of population, is a sovereign state. They also contended that while there may certainly, on occasion, be divisions on grounds of interest between groups of Member States, it is artificial to suppose that Member States would divide solely on the basis of size; nor is it likely that smaller Member States as such would act as a bloc in opposition to the interests of their larger partners either now or in a future enlarged Union.

The size and structure of the Commission

16.14   A further point of debate throughout the negotiations was the size and structure of the Commission and the powers of its President.

16.15   At present the Commission has twenty members. Article 157 of the EC Treaty and equivalent provisions in the other two Community Treaties, provide that the Commission must include at least one, and not more than two, nationals of each Member State. This means in practice, that the smaller Member State nominate one member each to the Commission and the five largest Member States (France, Germany, Italy, UK and Spain) nominate two each.

16.16   The person to be appointed President of the Commission is nominated by the Member Governments *"by common accord"*, after consulting the European Parliament. The Governments nominate the other Commission members, *"in consultation with"* the nominee for President. All of the members of the proposed Commission are then subject as a body to a vote of approval by the Parliament; and, once the Parliament has approved, they are formally appointed *"by common accord"* of the Governments.

16.17   The President of the Commission has status and prestige as the person who presides over its work but the actual authority attaching to the office as such is limited. He/she is essentially, so far as the other Commissioners are concerned, no more than first among equals. The Treaties also allow the Commission to appoint one or two Vice-Presidents from among its members.

16.18   During the negotiation of the new Treaty, some Member States argued that with a membership of twenty, the Commission is already too large to be effective; and that with more members added as the membership of the Union increases further it would become quite unwieldy.

16.19   Other Member States strongly disputed this view. They emphasised the key role of the Commission in the institutional structure of the Union as initiator, as administrator and as guardian of the Treaties. They argued that a strong Commission whose impartiality is accepted by the public in all Member States is vital to the political health and the progress of the Union; and that the Commission will be effective and its actions will be widely accepted only if it includes at least one national of each Member State.

16.20   There was general agreement that it would, in any case, be desirable to strengthen the status and the political authority of the President of the Commission.

16.21   The way in which these issues are dealt with in the new Treaty will be described further below.

Protocol on the Institutions

16.22   The issues of the size of the Commission and the weighting of votes in the Council were the subject of a compromise at the conclusion of the negotiations in Amsterdam. This compromise was embodied in a Protocol which is to be attached to the relevant Treaties (the Treaty on European Union and the

Treaties establishing the European Community, the European Coal and Steel Community and Euratom respectively).

What the Protocol will do

16.23 The effect of the provisions of the Protocol can be summarised as follows:

(i) there will be no change in the weighting of votes in the Council or in the size of the Commission until the next enlargement of the Union;

(ii) At the date when the first new Member States are admitted, the number of members of the Commission will be reduced to one per Member State. (At present each of the five largest Member States – France, Germany, Italy, Spain and UK – nominates two Members to the Commission.)

This provision is, however, conditional. It is based on the assumption that by that date there will have been a modification, acceptable to all Member States, in the voting rules in the Council. This modification may involve <u>either</u> a straight change in the weighting of votes <u>or</u> the introduction of a requirement for a dual majority. Whichever way it is done, "*all relevant elements*" must be taken into account – particularly the need to compensate each of the five large Member States for giving up the right to nominate a second member of the Commission;

(iii) At least a year before the number of Member States passes twenty (ie before the number of new Members admitted goes beyond five) another Intergovernmental Conference is to be called to carry out a comprehensive review of the Treaty provisions on the composition and functioning of the institutions.

16.24 It can be said, therefore, that the Protocol envisages the following sequence of events:

(i) There will be no immediate change;

(ii) At some point before the first new Members are admitted there will have to be an attempt made to get agreement on either a re-weighting of votes or the introduction of a dual majority requirement in the Council. This must lean towards the five large Member States to compensate them for giving up the right to nominate a second member of the Commission; and it must at the same time be acceptable to all Member States;

(iii) On the assumption that such an agreement has been reached by the date of the admission of the first new Members, the five large Member States will each give up the right to nominate a second Commissioner. This will reduce the size of the Commission to fifteen, plus one for each newly admitted Member State. For example, if three new Member States are admitted then the Commission will have a total of eighteen members (There is an implied assumption that the first wave of new entrants will not number more than five — see below);

(iv) At least a year before a sixth new Member is admitted (which would take the Union membership to twenty one or more), there will be another IGC to conduct a fundamental review of the Treaty provisions on the make-up and the working of the institutions. This, like every IGC, would work on the basis of unanimity. Nothing in the new Treaty pre-judges the outcome in any way.

Two points in these provisions may be noted: (a) the Treaty of Amsterdam will not affect the right of each Member State to nominate a full Member of the Commission; and (b) if it should be the case that the first new group of entrants to be admitted will number more than five, then the fundamental review envisaged in (iv) would begin at least a year before that date — that is a year before any enlargement of the Union takes place.

16.25   After the Amsterdam European Council in June and before signature of the Treaty on 2 October, three Member States — Belgium, France and Italy — made a Joint Declaration on the need to give full effect to this Protocol. They expressed the view that the results of the Intergovernmental Conference did not meet the need for substantial progress towards reinforcing the institutions and that such a reinforcement, which could take account also of the need for a significant extension of qualified majority voting, was an indispensable condition for conclusion of the first negotiations to admit new Members to the Union.

The European Parliament

Background

16.26   The European Parliament is the only directly-elected institution of the Community. In the negotiation of the new Treaty it was accepted by all that a strong and vigilant Parliament, acting on many issues as "co-legislator" with the Council in the adoption of Community legislation, is essential to a democratic Union.

16.27   Initially the powers of the Parliament within the institutional structure of the Community were weak but they have increased considerably over the years. The increase has been most marked since the system of direct election was introduced in 1979. The new Treaty strengthens these powers further as described below.

16.28   The Parliament has 626 members who are directly elected in the Member States in elections held every five years. As each group of new Member States has joined the Union, the number of seats in the Parliament has been increased proportionately. The allocation of seats as between Member States established in an Act of the Council of 1976 is now set out in Article 138 of the Treaty. Ireland elects 15 MEPs.

16.29   The method of election varies somewhat as between Member States but fourteen Member States operate some system of proportional representation. The UK maintains the "first past the post" system except for the three MEPs elected in Northern Ireland. The EC Treaty provides (Article 138.3) that the Parliament is to draw up proposals for elections by direct universal suffrage in accordance with a uniform procedure in all Member States. It will then be for the Council, acting unanimously with the assent of the Parliament, to decide on the system and to recommend that decision to Member States for adoption in accordance with their respective constitutional requirements. This has not yet been done.

Powers of the Parliament

16.30   The principal powers of the Parliament are legislative; budgetary; and powers in regard to international agreements.

Legislative procedures

16.31   The European Parliament does not have the power to enact legislation directly. What is described as its legislative power means in effect its role under the provisions of the EC Treaty in Community decision-making. There are four different procedures which involve the Parliament to a greater or lesser extent and one or other procedure is followed according to what the relevant Treaty article dealing with the matter in question prescribes.

16.32   The consultation procedure requires the Council to consult the Parliament but does not oblige it to accept the Parliament's opinion. The Parliament has, however, been able to gain leverage to influence proposals by exercising its ability to delay giving its opinion.

16.33   The cooperation procedure gives the Parliament a somewhat greater role although in the last resort, it still cannot block legislation. (Briefly, a "common position" adopted by the Council in response to a Commission proposal is referred to Parliament. If the Parliament amends it the Commission will re-examine the common position and refer it again to the Council. In the end the Council may adopt the proposal even if it is rejected by Parliament but only if it acts unanimously).

16.34   The co-decision procedure, introduced by the Maastricht Treaty in 1992 (as Article 189b of the EC Treaty) is intended to give the Parliament a real and substantial role as "co-legislator" with the Council in the areas where it applies.

16.35   As it has operated to date co-decision is a rather complex procedure which requires coordination and exchanges in regard to the content of pro-posed legislation between the Council and the Parliament and involves also the Commission. At a certain stage in the procedure, a Conciliation Committee with an equal number of members from the Council and the Parliament, works with the help of the Commission to achieve agreement. If agreement cannot be reached with the Council, however, then in the last resort, the Parliament, by an absolute majority of its members, may block the proposed legislation.

16.36   The assent procedure was introduced to the EC Treaty by the Single European Act of 1986 and extended by the Maastricht Treaty. It gives the Parlia-ment a veto in the areas where it applies such as, for example, in defining the tasks and priority objectives of the Structural Funds and in the conclusion of various kinds of international agreements. This means in effect that the Parlia-ment may veto such an agreement but may not amend its terms.

What the new Treaty will do

16.37   The main changes made by the new Treaty are in the legislative field. However, the budgetary role of the Parliament in regard to operational expendi-ture under the "Second Pillar" (Common Foreign and Security Policy) and the "Third Pillar" (Police and Judicial Cooperation in Criminal Matters) will also increase somewhat, since such expenditure will now normally be charged to the Community budget where the Parliament has a role. The new Treaty will also provide that the nomination of the person to be appointed President of the Commission "shall be approved by the European Parliament". The EC Treaty as it stands provides only that the governments of the Member States are to consult the Parliament on the nomination (Article 158.2).

16.38   The new Treaty will virtually abolish the cooperation procedure and thus reduce the number of legislative procedures involving the Parliament from four to three (consultation, co-decision and assent). In the course of the nego-tiations, however, it was decided that it would be important to make no change in the provisions in regard to Economic and Monetary Union already agreed in the Maastricht Treaty in 1992. For this reason the cooperation procedure has been retained wherever it is provided for in the section of the Treaty relating to EMU but otherwise it will disappear.

16.39   The new Treaty will provide for the use of co-decision in a substantial number of the new areas now to be introduced into the Treaty. In addition, it will also extend the co-decision procedure to areas to which consultation or cooperation now applies. The new Treaty will at the same time tighten up the procedure itself and simplify it somewhat, as well as giving the Parliament a somewhat stronger role in its final stages.

Extension of co-decision

16.40   The extension of the scope of co-decision in the new Treaty has been done by making individual provision for its application under the relevant articles dealing with decisions on various matters rather than by way of a single comprehensive article relating to the procedure itself. However, for ease of reference Appendix C to the present White Paper lists in tabular form the Articles of the EC Treaty to which the co-decision procedure will now apply.

Simplification of the co-decision procedure

16.41   The operation of the co-decision procedure has also been simplified to some extent by an amendment of Article 189b of the Treaty.

16.42   This will provide for some speeding up and streamlining of the procedure (and a Declaration calls on the European Parliament, the Council and the Commission to make every effort to ensure that the procedure operates as expeditiously as possible). Moreover, the procedure as revised, will place the Parliament on an equal footing with the Council in that it will remove the possibility which now exists that the Council may continue to seek to have a proposal adopted even if it has not proved possible for the Council to agree with the Parliament on a text in the joint committee (the so-called Conciliation Committee) which is provided for under the procedure.

16.43   In addition to these changes in the legislative procedures, the new Treaty will make three other changes involving the Parliament.

Limit on total membership of Parliament

16.44   The **first** is a provision that the number of members of the Parliament shall not exceed 700 (addition to Article 137 of the EC Treaty and equivalent provisions of the other Treaties). This is the first time an upper limit for the membership has been set. It means in effect that the number of seats in the Parliament will not be more than 700 no matter what changes may take place in the future in the membership of the Union.

16.45 In agreeing during the negotiations to introduce such a limit for the first time, the Member States had it in mind that any deliberative body such as the Parliament could become unwieldy and less effective if its membership continued to grow without limit. Since the membership at present is 626 there is "head-room" of some 74 seats available for allocation to new Members States before the limit of 700 which will now be set is reached.

16.46 If, as the Union expands by admitting more and more new Members a proportionate allocation of seats to each new Member would take the total beyond this limit, it will then become necessary to agree on a new allocation of seats in the Parliament as between all Member States. It was accepted during the negotiations, however, that any such future re-allocation could not be simply on a crude population basis only. It should take account of the need to ensure that, in a Union of Member States, every Member State as such will have an appropriate allocation of seats.

16.47 For this reason it has been agreed to add a provision to qualify Article 2 of the 1976 legislative Act where the allocation of seats as between Member States is set out. This addition provides that, in the event of changes in the present allocation, *"the number of representatives elected in each Member State must ensure appropriate representation of the peoples of the States brought together in the Community"*.

16.48 The safeguard for the position of smaller Member States which this provides will not become necessary until the addition of new Member States to the Union would involve the addition of more than 74 new seats to the Parliament. When that happens, however, and the upper limit of 700 comes into effect, the provision now added to the arrangements originally put in place by the 1976 Act will ensure protection for the smaller Member States whose seat allocation might otherwise be reduced below a threshold which they would consider acceptable.

Uniform procedure for direct elections throughout the Union

16.49 An amendment will also be made to the Articles of the Treaties which provide that the European Parliament shall draw up a proposal for direct elections in accordance with a uniform procedure in all Member States.

16.50 As explained in paragraph 16.29 above, fourteen Member States including Ireland, operate an electoral procedure based on some form of proportional representation and it is virtually certain that any uniform procedure to be adopted throughout the Community would also be based on some variant of that system. However, one Member State, the UK, has so far maintained the straight vote (first past the post) system except for the particular case of the three seats in the European Parliament allocated to Northern Ireland where a proportional representation system applies.

16.51 The change which is to be made by the new Treaty broadens the scope for the proposal which the Parliament is to make by adding to the phrase *"in accordance with a uniform procedure in all Member States"*, which is in Article 138.3, the wider phrase of *"or in accordance with principles common to all Member States"*. The intention of this was to open a better possibility of accommodation between different electoral systems in Member States.

Statute, conditions and rules for MEPs

16.52 The new Treaty will also add a provision to Article 138 which will allow the Parliament, after seeking an opinion from the Commission and with the unanimous approval of the Council, to lay down the regulations and general conditions which are to apply to its members in the performance of their duties.

Qualified Majority Voting

Background

16.53 While there was general agreement in principle on the part of all Member States to improve decision-making in the Council by extending the number of areas to which qualified majority voting applies, there was also some reluctance in practice on the part of many Member States to move from unanimity in particular areas.

16.54 Nevertheless some significant steps have been taken to extend the range of areas where qualified majority vote will henceforth apply. New provisions introduced to the EC Treaty by the Treaty of Amsterdam in fourteen areas will be subject to qualified majority voting and decisions in a number of other areas under existing articles of the Treaty will now also be taken by qualified majority rather than by unanimity.

What the new Treaty will do

16.55 A tabular statement showing all the changes in this regard in the EC Treaty is attached to the present White Paper as Appendix B. The new Treaty will also permit some use of qualified majority voting under the Common Foreign and Security Policy (the Second Pillar) and the Justice and Home Affairs provisions (the Third Pillar) of the Maastricht Treaty. These have been described in detail in Chapters 15 and 8 respectively of this White Paper.

What the new Treaty will do

Strengthening the role and status of the President

16.56   The new Treaty contains provisions designed to strengthen the authority of the President of the Commission within the collegiate structure of the Commission.

16.57   This will be done in three ways:

(i) the new Treaty will amend the provisions under which the European Parliament is to be consulted before the Governments of the Member States, by common accord, nominate a person to be President of the Commission. The new provision will require that *"the nomination shall be approved by the European Parliament."*

Since the nomination of the President of the Commission will have been specifically approved, not only by the Member Governments but by a vote in the Parliament before the other members of the Commission are appointed, the effect of this provision should be to strengthen the political authority of the President vis-a-vis the other members.

(ii) The Treaties provide at present that the Governments of the Member States shall nominate the other Members of the Commission *"in consultation with the nominee for President"*. This will be amended to read *"by common accord with the nominee for President"*.

The College of Commissioners as a whole will remain subject, as at present, to approval by the Parliament. It was not felt desirable to subject the other members of the Commission individually to approval by the Parliament as it was felt that this would tend to weaken the sense of collective responsibility and the collegiate character of the Commission as such;

(iii) The authority of the President of the Commission will also be strengthened by the addition of a new provision to Article 163 of the EC Treaty and equivalent Articles in the other Treaties. It will provide that *"the Commission shall work under the political guidance of its President"*;

Internal reorganisation of the Commission

16.58   During the negotiation of the Treaty, the President of the Commission informed the Conference that the Commission itself intended to prepare a reorganisation of tasks within the College in good time for the Commission which is to take office in the year 2000. This re-organisation is expected to involve allocation of specific tasks as well as conventional portfolios within the Commission.

16.59   Accordingly, a Declaration was agreed by the Member States in which they take note of the Commission's intention and express the view that the President of the Commission must enjoy broad discretion in the allocation of tasks within the College as well as in any re-shuffling of those tasks during a Commission's term of office. The Declaration notes also that the Commission intends to undertake in parallel a corresponding re-organisation of its Departments.

16.60   At present responsibility for various aspects of external relations is divided between a number of Commissioners. It is fairly widely accepted that greater coherence could be achieved through some concentration of responsibility. For this reason the Member States in the Declaration have also noted that it would be desirable to bring external relations under the responsibility of a Vice-President.

Jurisdiction of the Court of Justice

Background

16.61   The EU Treaty contains an Article (L) restricting the jurisdiction of the Court to certain provisions of that Treaty. The effect in practice is that the jurisdiction of the Court does not extend to the Common Foreign and Security Policy (the Second Pillar) or to Cooperation in Justice and Home Affairs (Third Pillar) except insofar as a convention adopted under the Third Pillar may stipulate that the Court shall have jurisdiction to interpret its provisions and to rule on disputes regarding its application.

What the new Treaty will do

16.62   The new Treaty will amend this Article in such a way as to extend the jurisdiction of the Court in relation to the provisions of the EU Treaty in three respects:

(i) The Court's jurisdiction will now extend, in principle, to the provisions on Police and Judicial Cooperation in Criminal matters (Third Pillar) in the ways and to the extent explained in Chapter 8 above.

This means that the Court will have jurisdiction to give preliminary rulings on the validity and interpretation of framework and other decisions under the Third Pillar; on the interpretation of conventions; and on the validity and the interpretation of measures implementing

Conventions. It will also have jurisdiction to review the legality of acts adopted under the Third Pillar and to rule on any dispute between Member States regarding the interpretation or application of such acts whenever the dispute cannot be settled by the Council within six months. The Court will also have jurisdiction to rule on any dispute between Member States and the Commission regarding the interpretation or the application of conventions;

(ii) The EU Treaty already provides (Article F) that the Union shall respect human rights as guaranteed by the European Convention on Human Rights, 1950, and as they result from the constitutional traditions common to the Member States as general principles of Community law. This provision is not, however, at present subject to the jurisdiction of the Court of Justice, although the Court has applied it in practice in its case law. The new Treaty will explicitly allow the Court of Justice, wherever it has jurisdiction under the Treaties, to apply these human rights principles to actions of the institutions.

(iii) The Court will have jurisdiction in relation to the new title VIa of the EU Treaty where the general rules which are to govern "closer cooperation" (sometimes called "flexibility") are set out ("Closer cooperation" is explained in detail in Chapter 17 of this White Paper.) This jurisdiction of the Court is made subject to the terms of Article 5a of the EC Treaty, the new Article which sets out the framework for "closer cooperation" in First Pillar matters; and to Article K.12 of the EU Treaty which will govern "closer cooperation" under the Third Pillar (This latter Article provides explicitly that the Court is to have jurisdiction in regard to the broad conditions to be met and the procedure to be followed in authorising "closer cooperation", as well as in regard to the procedure which will allow Member States not initially involved to join later).

The net effect in practice of these provisions is that the Court will have jurisdiction to ensure that the rules which are to govern "closer cooperation" under the First and Third Pillars are complied with (There is no provision for "closer cooperation" under the Second Pillar).

The Court of Auditors

Background

16.63   The Court of Auditors is a separate Community institution established by the Treaties to carry out the function of external financial auditor of expenditure by the institutions of the Community. The Court consists of one member appointed from each Member State and it has a staff of about 400.

16.64　The new Treaty strengthens the role of the Court of Auditors in certain ways without changing its basic functions.

What the new Treaty will do

Status

16.65　The formal status of the Court of Auditors as an institution will be emphasised by its being specifically mentioned in Article E of the EC Treaty along with the European Parliament, the Council, the Commission and the Court of Justice.

Right to take action in the Court of Justice

16.66　Under Article 173 of the EC Treaty and equivalent provisions in the other Community Treaties, the Court of Justice has jurisdiction in actions brought by the European Parliament and the European Central Bank for the purpose of protecting their prerogatives. The Court of Auditors will now also be explicitly mentioned in this provision. The effect will be that the Court of Auditors will be empowered to take action before the Court of Justice if it believes that its powers and prerogatives as provided for in the Treaties are being called into question.

Auditing the Accounts

16.67　Further amendments to the Treaties relate to the "statement of assurance" which the Court of Auditors is required to provide to the European Parliament and the Council as to the reliability of the accounts and the legality and regularity of the underlying transactions. The amendment to Article 188c of the EC Treaty and equivalent provisions in the other Community Treaties will provide that this statement is to be published in the Official Journal of the European Communities. An amendment to Article 206 (and equivalents) will include this statement as part of the material which the Council and the European Parliament are to examine in acting to give a discharge to the Commission in respect of the implementation of the budget.

16.68　Another amendment will be made to the provisions which require the Court of Auditors to examine whether all revenue has been received and all expenditure incurred in a lawful and regular manner and whether financial management has been sound. The new Treaty will add a requirement that the Court of Auditors report in particular on any case of irregularity.

16.69　An amendment will also be made to the provisions which specify that the audit is to be based on records and, if necessary, performed on the spot in the other institutions of the Community. The new Treaty will amend these provisions to allow the audit to be carried out also on the premises of any body which manages revenue or expenditure on behalf of the Community and in the Member States, including on the premises of any natural or legal person in receipt of payments from the Budget. Any such bodies or persons, like the institutions of the Community and the national audit bodies or competent Departments, will now be required to supply any document or information requested by the Court of Auditors. The Court of Auditors and the national audit bodies of the Member States are to cooperate in a spirit of trust while maintaining their independence.

16.70   Another amendment made by the new Treaty will provide that the right of access by the Court of Auditors to information held by the European Investment Bank (EIB) in connection with its activity in managing Community expenditure and revenue shall be governed by an agreement between the Court of Auditors, the Bank and the Commission. In the absence of an agreement the Court of Auditors shall nevertheless have access to information necessary for the audit of Community expenditure and revenue managed by the Bank. In a Declaration, the Member States invite the Court of Auditors, the EIB and the Commission to maintain in force the present tri-partite agreement.

The Economic and Social Committee

Background

16.71   The Economic and Social Committee is an advisory body established under the EC and Euratom Treaties. It consists of representatives of various categories of social and economic activity. Its members, together with an equal number of substitutes, are appointed by the Council, acting unanimously, for a term of four years. Ireland has nine members out of a total of 222.

What the new Treaty will do

16.72   The new Treaty will strengthen somewhat the consultative role of the Economic and Social Committee. The new provisions which are to be inserted in the EC Treaty in relation to employment, social matters and public health will require that the Economic and Social Committee be consulted on certain aspects of these issues (see details under the relevant headings elsewhere in this White Paper). A provision which will allow it to be consulted by the European Parliament has also been added to Article 198 of the EC Treaty.

The Committee of the Regions

Background

16.73   The Committee of the Regions is a body with advisory status consisting of representatives of regional and local bodies. It has a total membership of 222. There are nine Irish members, the same number as the Economic and Social Committee. Members of the Committee and alternates are appointed by the Council, acting unanimously, on proposals from the respective Member States.

What the new Treaty will do

16.74   Some steps have been taken in the new Treaty to strengthen the position of the Committee of the Regions. In establishing the Committee, the Maastricht Treaty in 1992 provided by a Protocol attached to the EC Treaty that the Economic and Social Committee and the Committee of the Regions should have a common organizational structure. The new Treaty provides that this Protocol shall be repealed. The effect is to free the Committee of the Regions from the linkage with the Economic and Social Committee which it had found limiting and to allow it to establish its own secretariat and organizational structure.

16.75   Some other amendments in relation to the Committee have also been made. One is an amendment to the Treaty provisions in regard to the appointment of members of the Committee (Article 198a). It will now stipulate that no member of the Committee shall at the same time be a member of the European Parliament.

16.76   The Committee is also to have power in future to adopt its own rules of procedure. This will be done by deleting from Article 198b of the EC Treaty a requirement that the rules of procedure are to be submitted for approval to the Council.

Extension of areas for consultation

16.77   The provision in the EC Treaty which requires the Committee of the Regions to be consulted by the Council and by the Commission in certain circumstances (Article 198c) will now have added to it by the new Treaty a reference pointing to matters concerning cross-border cooperation as particularly appropriate areas for consultation. Furthermore a new provision added to this Article will allow the Committee of the Regions to be consulted also by the European Parliament.

16.78   There are also a number of new provisions added to the EC Treaty by the new Treaty of Amsterdam which will require the Committee of the Regions to be consulted on aspects of the matters in question. These include provisions in regard to employment, social matters and the social fund, public health, environment, vocational training and transport.

Budget

What the new Treaty will do

16.79   No major revisions to the Community budgetary procedure will result from the new Treaty. However, operational expenditure arising under the Common Foreign and Security Policy, that is the Second Pillar (except for expenditure arising from operations having military or defence implications) and Police and Judicial cooperation in Criminal matters (Third Pillar) will now normally be charged to the Community Budget unless otherwise decided (see paragraphs 15.31 to 15.34 and 8.50 respectively). An Inter-Institutional Agreement with the Parliament (as explained in paragraphs 15.34 and 15.35 above) will govern the financing of the CFSP. In addition, the provision in Article 205 of the EC Treaty for the implementation of the Budget by the Commission will have added to it a provision requiring Member States to cooperate with the Commission to ensure that the Budget appropriations are used in accordance with the principles of sound financial management.

Procedure in relation to implementing powers of the Commission — Comitology

Background

16.80   Under the EC Treaty the Commission has law-making powers of decision in certain matters as of right and it also exercises the powers delegated to it by the Council for the implementation of Community law. The latter aspect of the Commission's activities is subject to the supervision of Committees composed of national experts with a Commission official in the chair.

16.81   There has been a particular growth in the number of such Committees because of the amount of technical legislation required by the Single Market programme put in place by the Single European Act of 1986. In 1987 the Council adopted a decision which, among other things, stipulates that there are three types of Committee: advisory, management and regulatory.

16.82 The European Parliament has expressed dissatisfaction with these arrangements which have come to be known as "comitology" . The new Treaty does not address the issue directly but in a Declaration the Member States call on the Commission to submit to the Council by the end of 1998 at the latest a proposal to amend the earlier Council decision of 1987.

Seats of Institutions and other bodies

What the new Treaty will do

16.83   The new Treaty will add to the EU Treaty and to the three Community Treaties a Protocol stipulating explicitly *"the location of the seats of the institutions and of certain bodies and departments of the European Communities and of Europol"*. It confirms the existing arrangements.

16.84   The Protocol provides that the Commission, the Committee of the Regions, the Economic and Social Committee and the Council will have their seats in Brussels but during the months of April, June and October, the Council is to hold its meetings in Luxembourg. The Court of Justice, the Court of First Instance, the Court of Auditors and the European Investment Bank are to have their seats in Luxembourg. The European Monetary Institute and the European Central Bank will have their seats in Frankfurt and Europol (the European Police Office) is to have its seat in The Hague.

16.85   The Protocol embodies in legal form a compromise (which was agreed some time ago and which is already being operated) in relation to the seat of the Parliament − an issue which had been a matter of contention between Belgium, France and Luxembourg. The Parliament is to have its seat in Strasbourg and it will hold the twelve monthly plenary sessions, including the Budget session, there. Additional plenary sessions and meetings of Committees are to be held in Brussels. The General Secretariat of the Parliament is to remain in Luxembourg.

Role of National Parliaments

Background

16.86   It is generally agreed that National Parliaments play their part in the democratic life of the Union primarily through holding the Governments of

Member States responsible and accountable at national level. Some Member States were concerned, however, to secure better recognition of the importance of the role of National Parliaments in the life and work of the Union. At the same time, there was general agreement that it would not be desirable to create a new Community institution.

What the new Treaty will do

16.87   The new Treaty will add a Protocol to the EU Treaty and to the three Community Treaties on the role of National Parliaments. This Protocol focuses in particular on two aspects: (i) information for National Parliaments and (ii) the role of the Conference of European Affairs Committees, known as COSAC, which was established in 1989.

Improved information for national parliaments

16.88   In providing for improved information for National Parliaments, the Protocol stipulates that all Commission consultation documents (Green and White Papers and communications) are to be promptly forwarded to National Parliaments; that Commission proposals for legislation are to be available in good time so that each Government may ensure that its own National Parliament receives them as appropriate; and that a six week period should elapse between the date a proposal is made available in all languages by the Commission to the European Parliament and the Council and the date when it is placed on the Council agenda for decision, subject to exceptions for cases of urgency.

Role for COSAC

16.89   The Protocol also provides that COSAC, which brings together representatives of European Affairs Committees of National Parliaments of the Member States, may make any contribution it deems appropriate for the attention of the institutions of the Union; it may examine any legislative proposal or initiative in relation to the establishment of an area of freedom, security and justice which might have a direct bearing on the rights and freedoms of individuals; and it may also address to the European Parliament, the Council and the Commission any contribution which it considers appropriate on the legislative activities of the Union particularly in relation to the application of the principle of subsidiarity and to the area of freedom, security and justice, as well as questions regarding fundamental rights. It is clearly stipulated also that the views made available by COSAC shall not bind the National Parliaments or pre-judge their position.

Role of Secretary General as High Representative for CFSP

16.90   During the negotiations there was considerable debate about a proposal which had been made that the European Council should appoint a "High Representative for the Common Foreign and Security Policy" with an extended mandate to take on a representational role and give the CFSP a higher international profile. In the event, however, as explained in paragraph 15.25, it was agreed that the task of "High Representative" should be entrusted to the Secretary General of the Council. Appropriate amendments will be made to the EU Treaty (Article J.16), to the EC Treaty (Article 151) and to the other Community Treaties.

16.91   The role to be given to the Secretary General as "High Representative" is described in Chapter 14 paragraphs 15.25 to 15.27). It was clear that if the Secretary General took on this new role, he/she would require assistance in carrying out the other functions involved in running the Secretariat. Accordingly, the new Treaty will provide, in an amendment to Article 157 and corresponding Articles in the other Community Treaties, that a Deputy will be appointed. Both will be appointed by unanimous decision of the Council.

CHAPTER SEVENTEEN

Closer Cooperation (Flexibility)

Summary

17.1 The possible addition to the Treaties of general provisions allowing "flexibility" or "closer cooperation" between a number of Member States short of the full membership who would be permitted to use the institutions of the Union was debated at some length during the negotiations which led up to the new Treaty.

17.2 The outcome has been that such "closer cooperation", subject to a considerable number of qualifications, will be permitted under new provisions to be added to the EC Treaty (First Pillar) and to the provisions on Police and Judicial Cooperation in Criminal Matters (Third Pillar) of the EU Treaty. No similar provisions (beyond the new provision for "constructive abstention" which could be considered a kind of flexibility) will be added to the Common Foreign and Security Policy (Second Pillar) section of the EU Treaty; nor will any provision of this kind be added to the two other Community Treaties which deal with the Coal and Steel Community and Euratom respectively. These provisions are explained in greater detail below.

Background

17.3 In specific and defined areas the EC Treaty already includes some provisions which permit a differentiated approach to integration or progress, for a certain time at least, at different speeds. Examples of this would be the periods of transition before the Treaty obligations apply in full which have been allowed in many cases to new Member States in their Accession Treaties; and the provisions in relation to Economic and Monetary Union which were added to the EC Treaty by the Maastricht Treaty and which envisage that, for a time at least, and perhaps indefinitely, a number of Member States less than the full membership will participate while the rest do not.

17.4 In the negotiation of the new Treaty, however, the point at issue was whether provisions on the lines of those applying to EMU should now be generalised so that on future occasions they could be applied in other areas not as yet specified or even perhaps foreseen.

Reasons for change

17.5   The argument for this was that the Member States of a future enlarged Union, with a membership of perhaps twenty five or more, may not all be able, or may not all be willing, to move forward together to greater integration in particular areas and that some further "flexibility" arrangements beyond the usual transition periods should be in place so that they might be invoked at that time. There might also be a possibility that Member States involved in EMU would wish to avail of general flexibility provisions to develop closer cooperation between themselves in other areas.

17.6   On the other hand, it could also be argued that the introduction of general "flexibility" provisions could be damaging to the coherence and the solidarity of the Union and could even over time have a "disintegrating" effect. This might happen if several different frameworks of cooperation each involving the institutions of the Union were to develop between somewhat different groups of Member States. To avert such a danger it would be necessary to impose limits and set a tight framework of rules to govern the circumstances in which the new provisions might be invoked.

What the new Treaty will do

17.7   The new Treaty will for the first time introduce to the Treaties a series of general provisions which will permit a number of Member States less than the full membership to avail of the institutions of the Union to organise "closer cooperation" between themselves (The term used is "closer cooperation" rather than "flexibility"). No pre-set number of participants is prescribed other than that the cooperation must involve at least a majority of the whole membership; and the provisions are general in the sense that the area or subject matter where they may be used is not specified, although certain areas have been explicitly excluded.

17.8   The new Treaty will insert provisions to this effect at three points in the overall Treaty system of the Union:

   (i) A new Title VIa containing three new articles will be added to the EU Treaty (Maastricht Treaty). It sets out what might be called the general rules which will govern "closer cooperation" in all cases;

   (ii) A new Article (5a) will be added to the EC Treaty to govern "closer cooperation" in Community matters (First Pillar);

   (iii) A new Article (K 12) will be added to the EU Treaty Title VI to govern closer cooperation in Police and Judicial Cooperation in Criminal Matters (Third Pillar).

17.9   As noted above no provision is made for "closer cooperation" as such under the Common Foreign and Security Policy (Second Pillar) although, under a new provision for "constructive abstention", a Member State may allow a decision to be adopted as a decision of the Union without being bound to apply it or pay for it. (see paragraph 15.20 above).

17.10   Items (i) and (ii) above are explained in greater detail below. Item (iii) has already been explained in Chapter 8:

(i)   General rules – new Title VIa in the EU Treaty

17.11   The new provisions to be added to the EU Treaty allow Member States to make use of the institutions, procedures and mechanisms of the Treaties to establish closer cooperation between themselves provided eight general conditions are met. The cooperation must be aimed at furthering the objectives of the Union; it must respect the principles of the Treaties; and it is to be used only as a last resort.

17.12   The most important of the other conditions are: that it concerns at least a majority of Members; that it does not affect the "acquis communautaire" — that is the accumulated body of decisions and legislation of the Community; that it does not affect the competences, rights, obligations and interests of non-participating Member States; and that it is open to all Member States and allows them to join at any time provided they accept the basic decision in regard to the new area of cooperation and comply with the decisions already taken in the new framework.

17.13   Additional Articles provide that all Member States will be able to take part in the deliberations but only those involved in the new area of cooperation will take part in decisions. Appropriate adjustments are made in the operation of the unanimity and qualified majority rules. The cost of implementing decisions apart from administrative costs for the institutions will fall only on participating Member States unless the whole Council unanimously decides otherwise. The Council and the Commission are to keep the European Parliament regularly informed.

(ii)   Closer cooperation in the First Pillar – new Article 5a in EC Treaty

17.14   A new Article 5a will be added to the EC Treaty setting out further specific provisions to apply to closer cooperation in Community matters — that is under the First Pillar. It begins by establishing explicit limitations in five respects. The closer cooperation must not (a) concern areas of exclusive Community competence; (b) affect Community policies, actions or programmes; (c) concern the citizenship of the Union or discriminate between nationals of Member States; (d) go beyond the limits of Community powers under the Treaty; (e) constitute a discrimination or a restriction of trade or distort competition between Member States.

147

17.15   A decision to establish "closer cooperation" under the First Pillar will be made by qualified majority vote in the Council on the basis of a proposal by the Commission and after consulting the European Parliament. The initiative will thus remain with the Commission, as is appropriate under the First Pillar. Member States which wish to set up closer cooperation between themselves may ask the Commission to make such a proposal. However, the Commission retains discretion whether or not to do so. (The precise language used is *"Member States ..... may address a request to the Commission, which may submit a proposal to the Council to that effect."*) If the Commission decides not to submit a proposal, it will inform the Member States concerned of the reason.

17.16   In addition, an "emergency brake" will apply to the decision in the Council. This provision (which is similar to that which has been introduced in the CFSP (Second Pillar) in cases where qualified majority voting could henceforth apply — see paragraph 15.21 above) will allow any Member State, in the last resort, to block a request to set up closer cooperation. It provides that if a Member of the Council declares that it opposes the decision *"for important and stated reasons of national policy"* no vote will be taken. The proposal will fall as a result. A qualified majority in the Council could force the issue to the European Council level but the Member State opposed could still veto the decision since unanimity is required for decisions at that level.

17.17   If a Member State which has not participated in the "closer cooperation" seeks to join at a later stage, the Commission will first give an opinion to the Council within three months and then decide on the application and on any necessary arrangements within four months of the date it was submitted.

CHAPTER EIGHTEEN

Simplification and re-numbering

18.1 As explained in the Introduction to this White Paper the structure of the European Union, comprising as it does three "Pillars" one of which itself comprises three distinct Communities, is quite complex.

18.2 The network of legal instruments which establish that structure has also become quite complex even as a set of inter-linked documents: the basic Treaties establishing the three Communities have been amended in various ways over the years; and they must now be read in conjunction with the EU Treaty (the Maastricht Treaty) which, in addition to amending these Treaties, added two new "Pillars" and established the whole structure as the European Union. The new Treaty, if ratified, will add to this complexity by making changes to all four of the Treaties and adding various Protocols to them.

18.3 Because of this it was agreed that the new Treaty should be used as an opportunity to achieve some simplification in the presentation of the Treaties. This will not change the fundamental structure of the Union based on three Pillars, as described in this White Paper. However, it will simplify the Treaties on which that structure is based by deleting obsolete articles in the three Community Treaties. The necessary legal enactments to give legal effect to these changes and adaptations, set out as Articles 6 to 11, constitute Part Two of the new Treaty of Amsterdam. Article 12 of the new Treaty provides for the re-numbering of the articles of the EU and EC Treaties but not the other two Community Treaties.

Simplification

18.4 The aim of simplification was to make the Treaties somewhat more readable — not to change the structure of the Union or of the Communities. It was accepted as a fundamental principle that what was being done should be done "on the basis of established law" — in other words that whatever was done should make no changes to the existing legal situation.

18.5 A full-scale re-drafting of the Treaty texts which might have made them more readable still was not undertaken. To have done so might have re-opened debate on provisions which were the outcome of detailed negotiations at various times in the past and which reflected compromises agreed with difficulty between the Member States at a particular time. More generally it was felt that such an exercise could have under-minded the *"acquis communautaire"* which is the term commonly used for the accumulated body of Treaty provisions and Acts and decisions of various kinds reached over the years which now form what might be called the legal substance of the Union.

Deletion of obsolete Articles and consequential changes

18.6   In the course of simplification, some drafting changes have been made but they are limited in number. For the most part they are simply the changes which were necessary to adjust the wording of the Treaties following deletion of obsolete provisions. In some exceptional cases a change going some way beyond this has been made.

18.7   That part of the simplification exercise which deals with deletion of obsolete articles with necessary consequential changes, covers the three Community Treaties as well as the Annexes and Protocols which are attached to them. It was not extended to the various Declarations made when the Treaties were adopted, since it was felt that these were statements of their time made by the Member States and they should simply be left stand as they were made. Nor did the exercise cover the EU Treaty. That Treaty was signed only five years ago and it was not necessary to delete obsolete articles in the same way as was the case in the three Community Treaties which go back more than 40 years and have been much amended by subsequent Treaties.

Re-numbering of articles

18.8   The re-numbering of articles on the other hand was carried out in both the EU Treaty and the EC Treaty but not in the two other Community Treaties (the Coal and Steel Community and Euratom).

18.9   The existing system of numbering Treaty articles is both complex and varied.The existing system of numbering Treaty articles is both complex and varied. As it stands at present, the EU Treaty uses an alphabetical sequence as the basic way of identifying articles but at times it supplements this with numbers. The Treaty begins with Article A, Article B etc. but for the CFSP (Title V) or Justice and Home Affairs (Title VI) it adds numbers to the alphabetical denomination of articles. Thus, for example, the Articles dealing with the CFSP are numbered J.1 to J.11 and those covering Justice and Home Affairs are identified as K to K.9. The EC Treaty uses what is basically a numerical sequence running from Article 1 to Article 240 but within the system, because of various amendments over the years, letters have been added to identify various new articles inserted. For example the article dealing with co-decision with the Parliament is Article 189b (which is a separate article and not simply part b of Article

189), while Title XVI on Environment comprises three articles identified as Articles 130r, 130s and 130t respectively.

18.10   The new Treaty of Amsterdam will re-number all of the articles in each of these two Treaties in a straight-forward numerical sequence. The articles in the EU Treaty, taking into account the substantive amendments which the new Treaty itself will make, will run from Article 1 to Article 53; the articles in the EC Treaty will run from Article 1 to Article 314. This may be somewhat disconcerting at first to those who are very familiar with particular articles designated in the older style, but it should be easier to understand for those approaching the two Treaties for the first time.

Safeguard clause as to legal effects

18.11   The new Treaty contains a specific provision (Article 10) stating explicitly that the deletions and other adjustments now being made will not bring about any change in the legal effects of the provisions in question or of acts based on them or change the legal effects of the time limits which they lay down. Neither will these changes affect the Accession Treaties (that is the Treaties under which, at various times, new Member States were admitted to membership). Furthermore, a Declaration affirms that the changes made will not affect the cumulative body of decisions which is described as the *acquis communautaire*.

Consolidated texts to be published

18.12   The texts of the two Treaties (EU and EC) incorporating the various kinds of amendments thus made (that is the substantive amendments which are now to be made, the deletion of obsolete articles and the re-numbering of the remaining articles as just described) have been published. They are described as "consolidated versions" of the respective Treaties. They should be useful for convenient reference, but only the successive Treaties as actually signed and ratified, together with new Treaty of Amsterdam if it is ratified, will stand as the authentic legal texts constituting, cumulatively, the Treaty structure of the Union.

Codification for illustrative purposes only

18.13   During the negotiations a further exercise of codification of the Treaties was begun. This is quite distinct from what is described above as consolidation. It would involve a much more radical re-structuring of articles and, in the fullest sense, a consolidation of all of the Treaties into what would in effect be a single Treaty text. Some Member States favoured this but in the view of others it could create considerable difficulties in regard to the existing *acquis*, that is the accumulated body of Treaty provisions, acts and decisions of the Union and might re-open many settled issues. It was agreed, nevertheless, that the exercise could continue after the end of the Conference and that the outcome would be made public in due course, but that it would be made clear that this was being done for illustrative purposes only and that it would not have any legal standing.

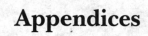

Appendices

APPENDIX A

Table of Equivalences
(See paragraphs 3.65 and 18.8)

A. Treaty on European Union

Previous numbering in the EU (Maastricht) Treaty	New numbering in the Consolidated Version of the EU Treaty
Title I	*Title I*
Article A	Article 1
Article B	Article 2
Article C	Article 3
Article D	Article 4
Article E	Article 5
Article F	Article 6
Article F.1 [1]	Article 7
Title II	*Title II*
Article G	Article 8
Title III	*Title III*
Article H	Article 9
Title IV	*Title IV*
Article I	Article 10
Title V [2]	*Title V*
Article J.1	Article 11
Article J.2	Article 12
Article J.3	Article 13
Article J.4	Article 14
Article J.5	Article 15
Article J.6	Article 16
Article J.7	Article 17
Article J.8	Article 18
Article J.9	Article 19
Article J.10	Article 20
Article J.11	Article 21
Article J.12	Article 22
Article J.13	Article 23
Article J.14	Article 24
Article J.15	Article 25
Article J.16	Article 26
Article J.17	Article 27
Article J.18	Article 28

[1] New Article introduced by the Treaty of Amsterdam.
[2] Title restructured by the Treaty of Amsterdam.

Previous numbering in the EU (Maastricht) Treaty	New numbering in the Consolidated Version of the EU Treaty
Title VI[2]	*Title VI*
Article K.1	Article 29
Article K.2	Article 30
Article K.3	Article 31
Article K.4	Article 32
Article K.5	Article 33
Article K.6	Article 34
Article K.7	Article 35
Article K.8	Article 36
Article K.9	Article 37
Article K.10	Article 38
Article K.11	Article 39
Article K.12	Article 40
Article K.13	Article 41
Article K.14	Article 42
Title VIA[3]	*Title VII*
Article K.15[1]	Article 43
Article K.16[1]	Article 44
Article K.17[1]	Article 45
Title VII	*Title VIII*
Article L	Article 46
Article M	Article 47
Article N	Article 48
Article O	Article 49
Article P	Article 50
Article Q	Article 51
Article R	Article 52
Article S	Article 53

[1] New Article introduced by the Treaty of Amsterdam.
[2] Title restructured by the Treaty of Amsterdam.
[3] New Title introduced by the Treaty of Amsterdam.

B. Treaty establishing the European Community

Previous numbering in the EC Treaty	New numbering in the Consolidated version of the EC Treaty
PART ONE	PART ONE
Article 1	Article 1
Article 2	Article 2
Article 3	Article 3
Article 3a	Article 4
Article 3b	Article 5
Article 3c[1]	Article 6
Article 4	Article 7
Article 4a	Article 8
Article 4b	Article 9
Article 5	Article 10
Article 5a[1]	Article 11
Article 6	Article 12
Article 6a[1]	Article 13
Article 7 (repealed)	–
Article 7a	Article 14
Article 7b (repealed)	–
Article 7c	Article 15
Article 7d[1]	Article 16
PART TWO	PART TWO
Article 8	Article 17
Article 8a	Article 18
Article 8b	Article 19
Article 8c	Article 20
Article 8d	Article 21
Article 8e	Article 22
PART THREE	PART THREE
Title I	*Title I*
Article 9	Article 23
Article 10	Article 24
Article 11 (repealed)	–
Chapter 1	Chapter 1
Section 1 (deleted)	–
Article 12	Article 25
Article 13 (repealed)	–
Article 14 (repealed)	–
Article 15 (repealed)	–
Article 16 (repealed	–
Article 17 (repealed)	–
Section 2 (deleted)	–
Article 18 (repealed)	–
Article 19 (repealed)	–

[1] New Article introduced by the Treaty of Amsterdam.

Previous numbering in the EC Treaty	New numbering in the Consolidated version of the EC Treaty
Article 20 (repealed)	—
Article 21 (repealed)	—
Article 22 (repealed)	—
Article 23 (repealed)	—
Article 24 (repealed)	—
Article 25 (repealed)	—
Article 26 (repealed)	—
Article 27 (repealed)	—
Article 28	Article 26
Article 29	Article 27
Chapter 2	Chapter 2
Article 30	Article 28
Article 31 (repealed)	—
Article 32 (repealed)	—
Article 33 (repealed)	—
Article 34	Article 29
Article 35 (repealed)	—
Article 36	Article 30
Article 37	Article 31
Title II	*Title II*
Article 38	Article 32
Article 39	Article 33
Article 40	Article 34
Article 41	Article 35
Article 42	Article 36
Article 43	Article 37
Article 44 (repealed)	—
Article 45 (repealed)	—
Article 46	Article 38
Article 47 (repealed)	—
Title III	*Title III*
Chapter 1	Chapter 1
Article 48	Article 39
Article 49	Article 40
Article 50	Article 41
Article 51	Article 42
Chapter 2	Chapter 2
Article 52	Article 43
Article 53 (repealed)	—
Article 54	Article 44
Article 55	Article 45
Article 56	Article 46
Article 57	Article 47
Article 58	Article 48

Previous numbering in the EC Treaty	New numbering in the Consolidated version of the EC Treaty
Chapter 3	Chapter 3
Article 59	Article 49
Article 60	Article 50
Article 61	Article 51
Article 62 (repealed)	—
Article 63	Article 52
Article 64	Article 53
Article 65	Article 54
Article 66	Article 55
Chapter 4	Chapter 4
Article 67 (repealed)	—
Article 68 (repealed)	—
Article 69 (repealed)	—
Article 70 (repealed)	—
Article 71 (repealed)	—
Article 72 (repealed)	—
Article 73 (repealed)	—
Article 73a (repealed)	—
Article 73b	Article 56
Article 73c	Article 57
Article 73d	Article 58
Article 73e (repealed)	—
Article 73f	Article 59
Article 73g	Article 60
Article 73h (repealed)	—
Title IIIa[3]	*Title IV*
Article 73i[1]	Article 61
Article 73j[1]	Article 62
Article 73k[1]	Article 63
Article 73l[1]	Article 64
Article 73m[1]	Article 65
Article 73n[1]	Article 66
Article 73o[1]	Article 67
Article 73p[1]	Article 68
Article 73q[1]	Article 69
Title IV	*Title V*
Article 74	Article 70
Article 75	Article 71
Article 76	Article 72
Article 77	Article 73
Article 78	Article 74
Article 79	Article 75
Article 80	Article 76
Article 81	Article 77
Article 82	Article 78
Article 83	Article 79
Article 84	Article 80

[1] New Article introduced by the Treaty of Amsterdam.
[3] New Title introduced by the Treaty of Amsterdam.

Previous numbering in the EC Treaty	New numbering in the Consolidated version of the EC Treaty
Title V	*Title VI*
Chapter 1	Chapter 1
Section 1	Section 1
Article 85	Article 81
Article 86	Article 82
Article 87	Article 83
Article 88	Article 84
Article 89	Article 85
Article 90	Article 86
Section 2 (deleted)	–
Article 91 (repealed)	–
Section 3	Section 2
Article 92	Article 87
Article 93	Article 88
Article 94	Article 89
Chapter 2	Chapter 2
Article 95	Article 90
Article 96	Article 91
Article 97 (repealed)	–
Article 98	Article 92
Article 99	Article 93
Chapter 3	Chapter 3
Article 100	Article 94
Article 100a	Article 95
Article 100b (repealed)	–
Article 100c (repealed)	–
Article 100d (repealed)	–
Article 101	Article 96
Article 102	Article 97
Title VI	*Title VII*
Chapter 1	Chapter 1
Article 102a	Article 98
Article 103	Article 99
Article 103a	Article 100
Article 104	Article 101
Article 104a	Article 102
Article 104b	Article 103
Article 104c	Article 104
Chapter 2	Chapter 2
Article 105	Article 105
Article 105a	Article 106
Article 106	Article 107
Article 107	Article 108
Article 108	Article 109
Article 108a	Article 110
Article 109	Article 111

Previous numbering in the EC Treaty	New numbering in the Consolidated version of the EC Treaty
Chapter 3	Chapter 3
Article 109a	Article 112
Article 109b	Article 113
Article 109c	Article 114
Article 109d	Article 115
Chapter 4	Chapter 4
Article 109e	Article 116
Article 109f	Article 117
Article 109g	Article 118
Article 109h	Article 119
Article 109i	Article 120
Article 109j	Article 121
Article 109k	Article 122
Article 1091	Article 123
Article 109m	Article 124
Title VIa[3]	*Title VIII*
Article 109n[1]	Article 125
Article 109o[1]	Article 126
Article 109p[1]	Article 127
Article 109q[1]	Article 128
Article 109r[1]	Article 129
Article 109s[1]	Article 130
Title VII	*Title IX*
Article 110	Article 131
Article 111 (repealed)	—
Article 112	Article 132
Article 113	Article 133
Article 114 (repealed)	—
Article 115	Article 134
Title VIIa[3]	*Title X*
Article 116[1]	Article 135
Title VIII	*Title XI*
Chapter 1[4]	Chapter 1
Article 117	Article 136
Article 118	Article 137
Article 118a	Article 138
Article 118b	Article 139
Article 118c	Article 140
Article 119	Article 141
Article 119a	Article 142
Article 120	Article 143
Article 121	Article 144
Article 122	Article 145

[1] New Article introduced by the Treaty of Amsterdam.
[3] New Title introduced by the Treaty of Amsterdam.
[4] Chapter 1 restructured by the Treaty of Amsterdam.

Previous numbering in the EC Treaty	New numbering in the Consolidated version of the EC Treaty
Chapter 2	Chapter 2
Article 123	Article 146
Article 124	Article 147
Article 125	Article 148
Chapter 3	Chapter 3
Article 126	Article 149
Article 127	Article 150
Title IX	*Title XII*
Article 128	Article 151
Title X	*Title XIII*
Article 129	Article 152
Title XI	*Title XIV*
Article 129a	Article 153
Title XII	*Title XV*
Article 129b	Article 154
Article 129c	Article 155
Article 129d	Article 156
Title XIII	*Title XVI*
Article 130	Article 157
Title XIV	*Title XVII*
Article 130a	Article 158
Article 130b	Article 159
Article 130c	Article 160
Article 130d	Article 161
Article 130e	Article 162
Title XV	*Title XVIII*
Article 130f	Article 163
Article 130g	Article 164
Article 130h	Article 165
Article 130i	Article 166
Article 130j	Article 167
Article 130k	Article 168
Article 130l	Article 169
Article 130m	Article 170
Article 130n	Article 171
Article 130o	Article 172
Article 130p	Article 173
Article 130q (repealed)	—

Previous numbering in the EC Treaty	New numbering in the Consolidated version of the EC Treaty
Title XVI	*Title XIX*
Article 130r	Article 174
Article 130s	Article 175
Article 130t	Article 176
Title XVII	*Title XX*
Article 130u	Article 177
Article 130v	Article 178
Article 130w	Article 179
Article 130x	Article 180
Article 130y	Article 181
PART FOUR	PART FOUR
Article 131	Article 182
Article 132	Article 183
Article 133	Article 184
Article 134	Article 185
Article 135	Article 186
Article 136	Article 187
Article 136a	Article 188
PART FIVE	PART FIVE
Title I	*Title I*
Chapter 1	Chapter 1
Section 1	Section 1
Article 137	Article 189
Article 138	Article 190
Article 138a	Article 191
Article 138b	Article 192
Article 138c	Article 193
Article 138d	Article 194
Article 138e	Article 195
Article 139	Article 196
Article 140	Article 197
Article 141	Article 198
Article 142	Article 199
Article 143	Article 200
Article 144	Article 201
Section 2	Section 2
Article 145	Article 202
Article 146	Article 203
Article 147	Article 204
Article 148	Article 205
Article 149 (repealed)	–
Article 150	Article 206
Article 151	Article 207
Article 152	Article 208
Article 153	Article 209
Article 154	Article 210

Previous numbering in the EC Treaty	New numbering in the Consolidated version of the EC Treaty
Section 3	Section 3
Article 155	Article 211
Article 156	Article 212
Article 157	Article 213
Article 158	Article 214
Article 159	Article 215
Article 160	Article 216
Article 161	Article 217
Article 162	Article 218
Article 163	Article 219
Section 4	Section 4
Article 164	Article 220
Article 165	Article 221
Article 166	Article 222
Article 167	Article 223
Article 168	Article 224
Article 168a	Article 225
Article 169	Article 226
Article 170	Article 227
Article 171	Article 228
Article 172	Article 229
Article 173	Article 230
Article 174	Article 231
Article 175	Article 232
Article 176	Article 233
Article 177	Article 234
Article 178	Article 235
Article 179	Article 236
Article 180	Article 237
Article 181	Article 238
Article 182	Article 239
Article 183	Article 240
Article 184	Article 241
Article 185	Article 242
Article 186	Article 243
Article 187	Article 244
Article 188	Article 245
Section 5	Section 5
Article 188a	Article 246
Article 188b	Article 247
Article 188c	Article 248
Chapter 2	Chapter 2
Article 189	Article 249
Article 189a	Article 250
Article 189b	Article 251
Article 189c	Article 252
Article 190	Article 253
Article 191	Article 254
Article 191a[1]	Article 255
Article 192	Article 256

[1] New Article introduced by the Treaty of Amsterdam.

Previous numbering in the EC Treaty	New numbering in the Consolidated version of the EC Treaty
Chapter 3	Chapter 3
Article 193	Article 257
Article 194	Article 258
Article 195	Article 259
Article 196	Article 260
Article 197	Article 261
Article 198	Article 262
Chapter 4	Chapter 4
Article 198a	Article 263
Article 198b	Article 264
Article 198c	Article 265
Chapter 5	Chapter 5
Article 198d	Article 266
Article 198e	Article 267
Title II	*Title II*
Article 199	Article 268
Article 200 (repealed)	—
Article 201	Article 269
Article 201a	Article 270
Article 202	Article 271
Article 203	Article 272
Article 204	Article 273
Article 205	Article 274
Article 205a	Article 275
Article 206	Article 276
Article 206a (repealed)	—
Article 207	Article 277
Article 208	Article 278
Article 209	Article 279
Article 209a	Article 280
PART SIX	PART SIX
Article 210	Article 281
Article 211	Article 282
Article 212[1]	Article 283
Article 213	Article 284
Article 213a[1]	Article 285
Article 213b[1]	Article 286
Article 214	Article 287
Article 215	Article 288
Article 216	Article 289
Article 217	Article 290
Article 218[1]	Article 291
Article 219	Article 292
Article 220	Article 293
Article 221	Article 294

[1] New Article introduced by the Treaty of Amsterdam.

Previous numbering in the EC Treaty	New numbering in the Consolidated version of the EC Treaty
Article 222	Article 295
Article 223	Article 296
Article 224	Article 297
Article 225	Article 298
Article 226 (repealed)	—
Article 227	Article 299
Article 228	Article 300
Article 228a	Article 301
Article 229	Article 302
Article 230	Article 303
Article 231	Article 304
Article 232	Article 305
Article 233	Article 306
Article 234	Article 307
Article 235	Article 308
Article 236 [1]	Article 309
Article 237 (repealed)	—
Article 238	Article 310
Article 239	Article 311
Article 240	Article 312
Article 241 (repealed)	—
Article 242 (repealed)	—
Article 243 (repealed)	—
Article 244 (repealed)	—
Article 245 (repealed)	—
Article 246 (repealed)	—
Final Provisions	**Final Provisions**
Article 247	Article 313
Article 248	Article 314

[1] New Article introduced by the Treaty of Amsterdam.

APPENDIX B

Application of Qualified Majority Voting

The following provisions, which will be introduced to the EC Treaty for the first time, will be subject to qualified majority voting:

Article 5a(2)	—	Closer cooperation - authorization
Article D(2), new Title on Free Movement	—	Provisional measures
Article 4, new Title on Employment	—	Employment guidelines
Article 5, new Title on Employment	—	Incentive measures
Article 118(2)	—	Social exclusion
Article 119(3)	—	Equality of opportunity and treatment of men and women
Article 129(4)	—	Public health
Article 191a	—	Transparency
Article 209a	—	Countering fraud
Article 213a	—	Statistics
Article 213b	—	Establishment of an independent advisory authority on data protection
Article 227(2)	—	Outermost regions
Article 236(2)(3)	—	Fundamental rights — sanctions
New Article	—	Customs cooperation

The following provisions, which already exist in the EC Treaty, will now be subject to qualified majority voting:

Article 45(3)	—	Compensatory aid for imports of raw materials
Article 56(2)	—	Coordination of provisions laid down by law, regulation or administrative action for special treatment for foreign nationals (right of establishment)

Article 130i(1)	—	Adoption of the research framework programme
Article 130i(2)	—	Adapting or supplementing the research framework programme
Article 130o	—	Setting up of joint undertakings in research & technological development

APPENDIX C

Application of the Codecision Procedure

The following provisions, which will be introduced to the EC Treaty for the first time, will be subject to the co-decision procedure:

Article (5)   —   Employment — Incentive measures

Article 118(2)
3rd subparagraph   —   Social exclusion

Article 119   —   Social policy — Equal opportunities and treatment

Article 129   —   Public health (former basis Article 43 — consultation)
                                    • minimum requirements regarding quality ˙ and safety of organs
                                    • veterinary and phytosanitary measures with the direct objective the protection of public health

Article 191a   —   General principles for transparency

Article 209a   —   Countering fraud affecting the financial interests of the Community

New Article   —   Customs cooperation

Article 213a   —   Statistics

Article 213b   —   Establishment of independent advisory authority on data protection

The following provisions, which already exist in the EC Treaty, will in future be subject to the co-decision procedure. The legislative procedure which currently applies is indicated in parentheses:

Article 6   —   Rules to prohibit discrimination on grounds of nationality (cooperation)

Article 8a(2)   —   Provisions for facilitating the exercise of citizens' right to move and reside freely within the territory of the Member States (assent)

Article 51	—	Internal market (consultation) • rules on social security for Community immigrant workers
Article 56(2)	—	Coordination of provisions laid down by law, regulation or administrative action for special treatment for foreign nationals [right of establishment]
Article 57(2)	—	Coordination of the provisions laid down by law, regulation or administrative action in Member States concerning the taking up and pursuit of activities as self-employed persons (consultation); Amendment of existing principles laid down by law governing the professions with respect to training and conditions of access for natural persons (consultation)
Article 75(1)	—	Transport policy (cooperation) • Common rules applicable to international transport to or from the territory of a Member State or passing across the territory of one or more Member States; • the conditions under which non-resident carriers may operate transport services within a Member State; • measures to improve transport safety; • other appropriate provisions.
Article 84	—	Transport policy (cooperation) • sea and air transport
Social policy	—	Articles resulting from the transposition into the Treaty of the agreement on social policy, except for aspects of that Agreement which are currently subject to unanimity (cooperation)
Article 125	—	Implementing decisions relating to the European Social Fund (cooperation)
Article 127(4)	—	Vocational training (cooperation) • Measures to contribute to the achievement of the objectives of Article 127
Article 129d	—	Other measures (TENs) (cooperation)
Article 130e	—	ERDF implementing decisions (cooperation)
Article 130o	—	Adoption of measures referred in Articles 130j, k and l - 2nd subparagraph [research] (cooperation)

Article 130s(1)   —   Environment (cooperation)
                         • Action by the Community in order to achieve
                           the objectives of Article 130r

Article 130w   —   Development cooperation (cooperation).

APPENDIX D

List of Protocols

Protocol annexed to the Treaty on European Union:

1. Protocol on Article J.7 of the Treaty on European Union

Protocols annexed to the Treaty on European Union and to the Treaty establishing the European Community:

2. Protocol integrating the Schengen acquis into the framework of the European Union

3. Protocol on the application of certain aspects of Article 7a of the Treaty establishing the European Community to the United Kingdom and to Ireland

4. Protocol on the position of the United Kingdom and Ireland

5. Protocol on the position of Denmark

Protocols annexed to the Treaty establishing the European Community:

6. Protocol on asylum for nationals of Member States of the European Union

7. Protocol on the application of the principles of subsidiarity and proportionality

8. Protocol on external relations of the Member States with regard to the crossing of external borders

9. Protocol on the system of public broadcasting in the Member States

10. Protocol on protection and welfare of animals

Protocols annexed to the Treaty on European Union and to the Treaties establishing the European Community, the European Coal and Steel Community and the European Atomic Energy Community

11. Protocol on the institutions with the prospect of enlargement of the European Union

12. Protocol on the location of the seats of the institutions and of certain bodies and departments of the European Communities

13. Protocol on the role of national parliaments in the European Union

APPENDIX E

List of Declarations

Declarations adopted by the Conference and annexed to the Final Act

1. Declaration on the abolition of the death penalty

2. Declaration on enhanced cooperation between the European Union and the Western European Union

3. Declaration relating to Western European Union

4. Declaration on Articles J.14 and K.10 of the Treaty on European Union

5. Declaration on Article J.15 of the Treaty on European Union

6. Declaration on the establishment of a policy planning and early warning unit

7. Declaration on Article K.2 of the Treaty on European Union

8. Declaration on Article K.3(e) of the Treaty on European Union

9. Declaration on Article K.6(2) of the Treaty on European Union

10. Declaration on Article K.7 of the Treaty on European Union

11. Declaration on the status of churches and non confessional organisations

12. Declaration on environmental impact assessments

13. Declaration on Article 7d of the Treaty establishing the European Community

14. Declaration on the repeal of Article 44 of the Treaty establishing the European Community

15. Declaration on the preservation of the level of protection and security provided by the Schengen acquis

16. Declaration on Article 73j(2)(b) of the Treaty establishing the European Community

17. Declaration on Article 73k of the Treaty establishing the European Community

18. Declaration on Article 73k(3)(a) of the Treaty establishing the European Community

173

19. Declaration on Article 73l(1) of the Treaty establishing the European Community

20. Declaration on Article 73m of the Treaty establishing the European Community

21. Declaration on Article 73o of the Treaty establishing the European Community

22. Declaration regarding persons with a disability

23. Declaration on incentive measures referred to in Article 109r of the Treaty establishing the European Community

24. Declaration on Article 109r of the Treaty establishing the European Community

25. Declaration on Article 118 of the Treaty establishing the European Community

26. Declaration on Article 118(2) of the Treaty establishing the European Community

27. Declaration on Article 118b(2) of the Treaty establishing the European Community

28. Declaration on Article 119(4) of the Treaty establishing the European Community

29. Declaration on sport

30. Declaration on island regions

31. Declaration relating to the Council Decision of 13 July 1987

32. Declaration on the organisation and functioning of the Commission

33. Declaration on Article 188c(3) of the Treaty establishing the European Community

34. Declaration on respect for time limits under the co-decision procedure

35. Declaration on Article 191a(1) of the Treaty establishing the European Community

36. Declaration on the Overseas Countries and Territories

37. Declaration on public credit institutions in Germany

38. Declaration on voluntary service activities

39. Declaration on the quality of the drafting of Community legislation

40. Declaration concerning the procedure for concluding international agreements by the European Coal and Steel Community

174

41. Declaration on the provisions relating to transparency, access to documents and the fight against fraud

42. Declaration on the consolidation of the Treaties

43. Declaration relating to the Protocol on the application of the principles of subsidiarity and proportionality

44. Declaration on Article 2 of the Protocol integrating the Schengen acquis into the framework of the European Union

45. Declaration on Article 4 of the Protocol integrating the Schengen acquis into the framework of the European Union

46. Declaration on Article 5 of the Protocol integrating the Schengen acquis into the framework of the European Union

47. Declaration on Article 6 of the Protocol integrating the Schengen acquis into the framework of the European Union

48. Declaration relating to the Protocol on asylum for nationals of Member States in the European Union

49. Declaration relating to subparagraph (d) of the Sole Article of the Protocol on asylum for nationals of Member States of the European Union

50. Declaration relating to the Protocol on the institutions with the prospect of enlargement of the European Union

51. Declaration on Article 10 of the Treaty of Amsterdam

Declarations noted by the Intergovernmental Conference and annexed to the Final Act

1. Declaration by Austria and Luxembourg on credit institutions

2. Declaration by Denmark relating to Article K.14 of the Treaty on European Union

3. Declaration by Germany, Austria and Belgium on subsidiarity

4. Declaration by Ireland on Article 3 of the Protocol on the position of the United Kingdom and Ireland

5. Declaration by Belgium on the Protocol on asylum for nationals of Member States of the European Union

6. Declaration by Belgium, France and Italy on the Protocol on the institutions with the prospect of enlargement of the European Union

7. Declaration by France concerning the situation of the overseas departments in the light of the Protocol integrating the Schengen *acquis* into the framework of the European Union

8. Declaration by Greece concerning the Declaration on the status of churches and non-confessional organisations

Wt. P46570. 6,000. 1/98. Cahill. (M26994). G.Spl.